A Heart to Heart With the Father

Devotional Series

*May Gods peace go with you as
you journey with Him.*

Clarice Fowler

Clarice Fowler

THE JOURNEY BEGINS

BOOK ONE

To order additional copies of this book, contact:
Xlibris Corporation
1-888-795-4274
www.Xlibris.com
Orders@Xlibris.com
90671

Contents

My heart's desire . . .

"The Lord directs the steps of the godly, He delights in every detail of their lives . . . by day the Lord directs His love, at night His song is with me . . . See how very much our Father loves us, for he calls us His children, and that is what we are! . . . How precious are Your thoughts about me, O God, they cannot be numbered."

Psalm 37:24, (NLT), Psalm 42:8, (NIV), I John 3:1 NIV). Psalm 139:12 (NLT).

His heart's promise . . .

"the very hairs on your head are numbered. So don't be afraid you are more valuable than many sparrows" . . . "I will instruct you and teach you in the way you should go, I will counsel you and watch over you . . . I will never fail you, I will never abandon you."

Luke 12:7, (NIV), Psalms 32:8, (NIV), Hebrews 13:5, (NLT).

Dedication

To Diana Ramsey

Without whom this writing would not exist.

You have felt the pulse of my heartbeat
as you read every page from my very first rough draft
and throughout each stage of this work.

You have been my strength and support system
through the mountains and the valleys of my soul search.
You are more than a friend . . .
You are my soul mate.

Thank you will never be enough.

Acknowledgements

I want to express my deepest gratitude to the following special people without whom this work would not have gone forward.

Millie Barger, *who took on this project when I was very green as a writer. With her help and skills, she carefully taught me and edited my work throughout the tedious blossoming of this endeavor. She has been my mainstay and strength as we have grown together in this work and in a friendship that only our Father could foretell.*

Rosalyn Christopher, *my editor for "The Journey Begins project. You have not only been my editor, but a true friend who has helped me not only on this work, but on many other ventures as well. I deeply appreciate all you do and all you are to me.*

Nelda Davis, *my project editor. Our meeting was ordained of the Lord who amazingly put us together at a Women's Retreat. Though we worship in different towns and live in different places, our meeting was destined to take place. Only the Lord knew how badly we needed each other. Thank you for your fine work as we labor together for our Lord.*

Chris Fowler, *my son, who by profession is a graphic artist. He willingly gave of his time and effort to produce the vision that I had for this cover and also guided and directed me in taking this project to its completion. How blessed I am to have a son with this kind of talent within my family!*

Don Fowler, *my husband, who had faith in me and kept me centered between work and rest for my body. His patience and perseverance sustained me as he painstakingly edited the scripture content through each of the various translations used.*

Jill Rhodes, *my daughter and counsel, who encouraged me spiritually and physically to do this work and helped me keep on, keeping on, when my spirit needed a boost. Her dedication to make sure that this work became a book (actually four books), helped me in the hard times of this work.*

Most of all, to my Lord and Savior Jesus Christ, *who taught me so much about Our Father in heaven. What a marvelous journey! So much farther above anything I could have envisioned for my life. All praise and honor to Him!*

Introduction

My journey began in 1994 to seek a deeper understanding of the person of God as my heavenly Father. I did not have a good earthly father image and I felt the need to explore and experience the very heart of my heavenly Father, more intimately.

I had been a Christian since I was six years old and had loved my Lord dearly, but I was at a point in my life where I longed to dig deeper into His heart until our hearts beat as one.

It was a particularly difficult time as my husband, Don, and I were drastically changing the course of our lives, and I did not have clear direction in knowing what God had in mind for us.

We found ourselves in a rather strange place for a married couple. We had always been available for our parents and had taken care of both sides as their health deteriorated. We were living about eighty miles away from my in-laws when we had to make the complex decision to have my mother-in-law removed from their home due to the progression of several mental diseases. My father-in-law was still in very good health for his eighty-five years, so my husband and I made the difficult commitment to make sure that we would personally take care of Dad for the rest of his life.

They lived in a mobile home in Salem, Oregon. We did not want to disrupt Dad's life any more than it already had been, so my husband moved in with his father for what we thought would be a short period. His home was not large enough for both of us to live full time and we had other obligations to fulfill, so I lived and maintained our residence in Newport Oregon. I was traveling back and forth through Salem anyway, as various activities and commitments frequently brought me there.

In 1999, my friend, Diana, bought me a devotional book for Christmas. I decided that I would keep it at my father-in-law's house and use it when I was in town. From the first day of the devotional, I started journaling the attributes and qualities of God, with the caption "God is" . . . This was not the topic of the devotional, but for some reason I remained faithful to the format, never thinking that God might use it in some way. I made notations every time I was in Salem throughout the year, 2000. (Little did I know that our lives were about to take another twist in the road.)

My husband and I felt led to get an apartment closer to Salem, so that we could be together more often. Why we did not look for something in Salem only our Father knows, but we were led to this neat little town named Dallas, about fifteen miles west of Salem.

After renting a triplex unit for a few months, one of the other units became available. Without hesitation, dad joyfully agreed to sell his home and move in next door to us. By the time we were able to complete the move, it was clear to both of us that dad was not strong enough to live alone. Therefore, the strangest phase of my marriage took place. I ended up living next door to my husband and father-in-law! We saw each other daily however, it felt very strange.

In 2002, a little over a year later, we bought a home in this wonderful Dallas community and moved dad in with us. During that period, I read other devotionals and studies. I had (this one) accessible, but for some reason I only wrote sporadically in 2003. I did not pick it up again for two years. It was a tremendous period of spiritual growth, as the Lord was working many things out in my life. Finally, in February 2005, I picked up (this devotional) and continued my quest.

As I was reading my notes, I was astounded to find that I had listed over two-hundred and fifty titles with the caption of "God is . . . ," so I continued with that format. On March 8, 2006, I felt a clear direction from my heavenly Father to start writing this book. It is amazing in and of itself, because I have never written a book in my life, nor had any desire to do so.

In June of 2008, after completing three-hundred and sixty five days of learning so much about my heavenly Father, I recognized what a massive undertaking God had so generously given me to write. After much prayer, counsel and thought, I realized that this work needed to be divided into four books, not just one. A new challenge had begun.

Finally, the path was clear. The Series was named "Heart to Heart with the Father." Book 1 is "The Journey Begins" It is the first ninety-one days of the original three hundred sixty five. The remaining three books as of now will be, Book Two: "A Seeking Heart," Book Three: "A Listening Heart" and Book Four: "A Responsive Heart."

Another unique element about this series is the presence of a sparrow on each cover. When I was still in my twenties, I lost two sisters in a head-on collision. During that horrible time, God gave me a song that has stayed with me to this day: "His Eye Is on the Sparrow." For over fifty years, this unique occurrence has been with me whenever I go through deep trials. The sparrow on the cover is to honor Him who has been so amazingly merciful to me.

I also wanted to make this devotional interactive, because that inspirational experience, which became interactive for me, has been a wonderful tool in the hands of God to use me in a way that is beyond my wildest dreams.

If you would like to write your thoughts, you have the opportunity to do so under the caption "Your Reflections." One of the many things I have learned through the completing of this work is that God has no limits on what or whom He can use if we are willing to be His vessel.

As you read this work, you will find how God is taking this raw, unknown woman who never wrote a book in her life and has begun to shape me from a very green writer to one that by the end of these four books is learning to be a usable vessel in the hands of my heavenly Father. My search to know His heart, not only is allowing me the privilege of having a closer relationship with Him spiritually, but also is making me into an author whom He will use for His purpose.

I am in my mid-seventies and never expected to be used by the Lord in this way; however, this has been a rich blessing and one of the most rewarding times in my life. All glory goes to my heavenly Father who is just waiting to mold and shape my heart to beat with His as I follow Him on this new journey.

Day 1

God is . . . All Powerful

Bible Reading: Psalm 66:1-7

On Christmas Day, 1999, I wrote, "Sometimes I go about my daily life taking God for granted. I know Him as my personal Savior, but I want a deeper understanding of who He really is and the power He displays. I am beginning to understand who I am because of Him. I want to know Him better and have a closer relationship with Him."

As I focus on God's omnipotence, there is nothing with which to compare it. Many experienced ministers and writers have written about this and probably all of the other subjects that I will cover, but somehow God chose me to do this work. This calling overwhelms me. These thoughts are only a reflection from my own personal experience as a child of this mighty God.

What is the epitome of human power? We look at some world leaders and see the authority they wield through their positions. Many times, they keep their people under bondage and terror as they seek to control their every move. Some are so egotistical in their domination that they erect monuments and statues of themselves. In fact, the Russian leader, Vladimir Lenin, is embalmed and on display in a glass coffin in Leningrad (city also named after him). We certainly have had more than our share of examples in the twentieth and already in the twenty first century.

The psalmist wrote, "For by His great power He rules forever. He watches every movement of the nations; let no rebel rise in defiance" Psalm 66:7 (NLT). I love this verse because even though our world is crazy right now and we face numerous threats from terrorists and evil in other world leaders, we can be confident that the God of the universe sees it all and His ultimate plan will prevail. What a comfort He is in troubling times!

God's mightiness is a secure and enduring source of love and grace that transcends anything that we could ever imagine. "For His unfailing love toward those who fear Him is as great as the height of the heavens above the earth" Psalm 103:11 (NLT).

Personal Note:

As I ponder this gentle God who is so loving and kind to all who have accepted Him, I know that He also rules with an iron fist those who are disobedient to His calling. Yet He is consistently fair and perfect in all of His dealings.

As I start giving you glimpses into my personal notes, I am hopeful that you will see the growth the Lord has performed in me. In addition, maybe someone along the way will be able to relate to where I was, where I am, and where I can be in relationship with this powerful God I serve! I am glad that I am able to call Him "Father!"

Prayer:

Father, You hold the world in Your hands and watch over the actions of every country, and nothing goes unnoticed by You. Thank you for giving me confidence in knowing that all things are in Your mighty hands, so I need not worry. I thank You because, even though You are all-powerful, You love me with a gentle love that surpasses anything that I could ever imagine. In Jesus' name, Amen.

Your Reflections:

Day 2

God is . . . Faithful

Bible Reading: Psalm 18:25-29

My husband Don and I have been married over fifty-five years. It is becoming more and more rare to see such long-term commitments. When I married at age eighteen, marriage was the ultimate goal for most young "ladies." We just wanted to be married, raise a family, stay home with the children, and remain faithful "'til death do us part."

Many marriage vows today, however, do not even include those words in them. In fact, many couples write their own vows to each other, and I think some are very beautiful and touching, but others have little or no commitment attached to them. Marriage, as I experienced it, is very old-fashioned and outdated. With so little commitment in our society, it is hard for some to understand this depth of promise to one another. We fall far short of what God considers faithful, let alone understanding His reliability in this. In the Psalms we read, "For the Lord is good. His unfailing love continues forever, and His faithfulness continues to each generation" Psalm 100:5 (NLT).

Wow! What a loving, mighty and faithful God we serve. "He will never leave us nor forsake us" Deuteronomy 31:6b (NIV). It takes His great strength and power to love us even when we are unlovable to Him. He will not walk away when we get angry with Him. He will never divorce us, or leave us, even when we leave Him.

This is a hard concept for us to imagine. Nevertheless, God does not ask us to understand His fidelity, He only asks us to step out in faith and accept it. "Understand, therefore, that the Lord your God is indeed God. He is the faithful God who keeps His covenant for a thousand generations and lavishes His unfailing love on those who love Him and obey His commands" Deuteronomy 7:9 (NLT). Faithful, unfailing love, what more could we want?

Personal Note:

No matter whether I am unwavering in my faith or not, God is always steadfast and ready to forgive me and help me grow stronger in Him. In addition, if I let Him, He will take me to heights and places that I never dreamed possible. He never fails me. Sometimes I can get so involved in my own busy life that I give little or no thought to Him. How rich my life is, however, when I talk to Him and get to know Him more intimately each day. What a blessing to know that He lavishes His love on me when I keep His commands. What a faithful God I serve!

Prayer:

Oh Father, thank You for your unchanging ways. Forgive my complacency; and teach me more about Your reliability. Help me to grow in You, that I may experience more of the richness of your love. In Jesus' name, Amen.

Your Reflections:

Day 3

God is . . . Ever-Present

Bible Reading: Psalm 9:4-10

In October 1998, I found out that I had breast cancer. There is something about hearing the word "cancer," connected to you that is startling! It knocks the props right out from under you. My best option was to have a complete mastectomy to make sure that I would have the best result possible.

Whenever we go through deep waters, like a death of a loved one, a life-threatening disease, a divorce or any other thing that is life-changing, we are always at a crossroad. We can choose to become bitter or better. It seems like it takes the hard times in life before we realize that God is always *there* for us. When things are going well, we sometimes get a little too busy for devotions or prayer; and pretty soon we find ourselves not as close to God as we were when we were going through our trial.

When we pray and yield our life anew and put the situation in God's hands, He will always bring us closer to Him. There is an old hymn titled, "He's Only a Prayer Away." God is present always! In good times or bad, He will unceasingly be there for us. Psalm 9:10 reads, "Those who know Your name will trust in You; for You, Lord, have never forsaken those who seek You" (NIV). What an awesome Scripture! Our God is ever-present. He will never forsake us!

Personal Note:

My decision was clear, I had the mastectomy and have been cancer-free now for over ten years and I know that God has a real purpose for my life. When you face something like cancer, you find out what is important. Family becomes more precious, priorities change; life, and how you live it, becomes of much greater value.

I think this event was also very instrumental in my quest to know my Father better. God is nearer to me than ever. One of my favorite verses is in the psalms: "God is our refuge and strength, an ever-present help in trouble" Psalm 46:1 (NIV). He is always right there to cherish me and hold me close so that I can weather whatever life brings me. There is nothing greater than that!

Prayer:

Oh Father, I praise You because You are always with me. Help me to seek Your presence with all of my heart as I learn more about You. Thank you for Your steadfast love. In Jesus' name, Amen.

Your Reflections:

Day 4

God is . . . Unshakable

Bible Reading: Hebrews 1:8-12

Remember Y2K? That was when we were sure that the computer world was going to crash around us and uncertainty was at a high peak. The hype was at a volatile level and the spirit of fear was all around us. Today I feel more unrest than ever, but I have comfort in knowing that God sees and knows everything. What a blessing this is in a world which is constantly changing. It is so unstable, and we have no security in anything around us. Since September 11, 2001, our lives have taken a dramatic turn, not only in America, but also around the world. Much of the world lives in constant terror.

We have been blessed in this country so far, because our principles have been founded on the Word of God. Nevertheless, much of that is changing. We pray for God's mercy to prevent any terrorist attacks, but we live with the constant threat. It is great to know that though everything is becoming consistently more unstable, our God is unshakable. "You, Lord, in the beginning laid the foundation of the earth, and the heavens are the work of Your hands. They will perish, but You remain" Hebrews 1:10,11a (NKJ).

Even though we live with unrest every day, it is wonderful to know that we do not have to worry. We serve an immovable God who holds the world in His hand and has everything in His control. His ultimate plan will prevail! "The Lord frustrates the plans of the nations and thwarts all their schemes" Psalm 33:10 (NLT).

No matter how insecure our surroundings feel, God has all things under His control and will fulfill His purpose for our land. He is a just God who knows everything and has a purpose for all things. In Revelation 3:1 John wrote, "You are worthy, O Lord, to receive glory and honor and power, for You created all things and by Your will they exist and were created." (NKJ). What a comfort!

Personal Note:

Paul wrote another verse that I love, "Therefore since we are receiving a kingdom that cannot be shaken, let us be thankful, and so worship God acceptably with reverence and awe" Hebrews 12:28 (NIV). No matter what terror and unrest surrounds me, I know that I can put my trust in my Father and that brings me peace and comfort. Thank goodness, I serve an unshakable God.

Prayer:

Oh Father, I praise You because You are steadfast in all Your ways. Help me to seek Your presence with all of my heart, in the good times as well as the bad, as I learn more about You. Thank you for Your steadfast love, which can never be shaken. In Jesus' name, Amen.

Your Reflections:

Day 5

God is . . . Unchanging

Bible Reading: Isaiah 55:6-12

God is our sure foundation; He is consistently immovable. His ways are so far above ours that too often we are confused because we feel like nothing is happening the way we planned it. Life never seems to "quite work."

The problem is that we are trying to make our lives work, rather than allowing God to work His awesome plan through us. Jeremiah wrote, "'For I know the plans that I have for you,' says the Lord. 'They are plans for good and not for disaster, to give you a future and a hope.'" Jeremiah 29:11 (NLT).

Why is it so hard for us to give up our flighty ways? Often we change our minds as often as we do our shoes. It is difficult to have a solid future with such a changeable, uncommitted attitude. I really believe that our society is messed up today due, in a large part, to our lack of commitment to almost anything and everything.

We are a very bored society. We change jobs frequently so that we can "climb another rung on the ladder" of success." We discard marriages because of "incompatibility." Anything that is the least bit distasteful we throw out like trash. It is hard for us to imagine the world of fifty years ago, let alone a century ago.

I recently saw a movie, *The Time Changer* that was a revelation to me. It took place in 1890 and featured a professor who was an innovative thinker. He wanted to loosen a few rules that "couldn't hurt anybody," but then a colleague who was an inventor of a time machine, finally moved him forward through time one hundred years. He saw for himself what compromise had done to the society.

We may try to change and weaken our resolve all we want, but we cannot improve on a perfect God who is rock-solid and unmovable, who we can count on for all of our needs. Malachi wrote, "I am the Lord, and I do not change" Malachi 3:6a (NLT). Now that is as clear as it gets!

Personal Note:

From my journal on New Year's Eve 1999: "The hype surrounding the turn of the century is electrifying. We are watching the whole world celebrate the birthing of the new century and they are doing it with huge fireworks displays all over the world. We still have some uncertainty concerning whether our electronic system is going to be successful in making all of the necessary changes to a new century, but it is looking more hopeful."

Little did I know that much worse was yet to face us less than two years in our future. The September 11, 2001 attack on our country changed us all.

Prayer:

Oh, my Father, I praise You and thank You that I can count on You in a world that is ever changing. I praise You that You are steady and unchangeable. Help me to learn to rely more on Your plan for my life. In Jesus' name, Amen.

Your Reflections:

Day 6

God is . . . In Charge

Bible Reading: Daniel 4:28-33

How arrogant we can become as human beings. God can bring kings as well as individuals to their knees if we show no regard for Him. Consider King Nebuchadnezzar who had thrown three of God's children into a fiery furnace yet they survived because God was with them. Afterwards, the King acknowledged God's power and authority. Daniel wrote, "It is my pleasure to tell you about the miraculous signs and wonders that the Most High God has performed for me. How great are His signs, how mighty His wonders! His kingdom is an eternal kingdom; His dominion endures from generation to generation" Daniel 4:2-3 (NIV).

It seems the King understood how mighty our God is! However, in the next verse, the king had a dream so terrifying that he called together all of his wise and talented magicians and diviners in the land and told them his dream, but no one could interpret it.

Finally, he called Daniel who told the king the bad news that God would take away his kingdom from him and that he would go insane. He would eat the grass of the fields like an animal and remain deranged until he would acknowledge that the Most High God is sovereign over the kingdoms of men.

It took the king seven years before he would bow his knee, as he lived like an animal on all fours, grazing like a cow. His hair grew as long as eagle's feathers and his nails looked like bird's claws. Finally, the king raised his eyes to heaven and really repented of his arrogance.

After he repented, God not only restored his kingdom, but it was even better than before. The king finally was able to give all praise and glory to our Creator, the God of heaven and earth. Daniel wrote, "After this time had passed I, Nebuchadnezzar, looked up to heaven. My sanity returned, and I praised and worshiped the Most High and honored the One who lives forever. His rule is everlasting and His kingdom is eternal" Daniel 4:34 (NLT). What a merciful God we serve!

Personal Note:

From my journal on January 1, 2000: "As we watched the whole world celebrate the turn of the century, my eyes have never seen such a celebration. However, not all the glamour and impressive fireworks can even come close to the beauty I will behold when I see the Ruler of the universe sitting on His throne and welcoming me to His eternal 'party!'" His kingdom will never end. God is definitely in charge!

Prayer:

Father, forgive me for sometimes forgetting that You are on the throne of my heart, taking things out of Your control and trying to do them myself. Lord, I confess my arrogance and I pray that You will take charge of my heart again and be my Most High God Almighty! In Jesus' name, I pray this, Amen.

Your Reflections:

Day 7

God is . . . A Righteous Judge

Bible Reading: Psalm 97:1-6, 10-12

When we think of a righteous judge, what comes to mind? If it is God who sits on His throne with a long gavel, waiting for us to do something wrong, then we have a false image of our amazing God. Isaiah 30:18 reads, "Yet the Lord longs to be gracious to you; He rises to show you compassion. For the Lord is a God of justice. Blessed are all who wait for Him" (NIV).

If we are in His family then His righteousness and justice protects us. Psalm 97 starts out very positive: "The Lord reigns, let the earth be glad; let the distant shores rejoice. Clouds and thick darkness surround Him; righteousness and justice are the foundation of His throne . . . Light is shed upon the righteous, and joy on the upright in heart" Psalm 97:1,2,11 (NIV). The Psalms are full of praise to our God who rules and reigns, and love and fairness that He gives to the upright in heart. Yes, our God judges righteously.

Many people in the world today believe that there is a God. Nevertheless, it is easier for them to ignore His power and intimacy. They want to disregard Him or just put Him on the back burner so that they can control their own lives. Many others rationalize that someday when they are old they might think more seriously about God.

People have had this same attitude since Adam and Eve sinned in the Garden of Eden. It is Satan's most effective tool! But oh, how it grieves our Heavenly Father. He has such a rich and full life for us if we will only lay hold of it and trust Him, yet He is a fair judge and if we choose to ignore Him, our time of judgment will come! The Psalmist wrote, "Tell all the nations, the Lord reigns! The world stands firm and cannot be shaken. He will judge all peoples fairly" Psalm 96:10 (NLT).

Personal Note:

How often I have failed to trust in my Father's plan for me. I am so grateful that He judges with mercy instead of merit, because no one can ever be righteous enough on his or her own. Jesus stands before our righteous God on our behalf; and the Father looks at us through Jesus' perfection. Then He forgives us, and keeps on forgiving and forgiving. His judgment is always fair and righteous and I am so thankful that it is!

Prayer:

Thank you, Father, for Your mercy and grace. I praise You that You judge righteously and I thank You for Jesus who took my place so that I may stand before You through His perfection. I praise You with all of my heart. In His name, Amen.

Your Reflections:

Day 8

God is . . . Above Our Ways

Bible Reading: Psalm 139:1-17

It is very hard sometimes to understand God's ways and plans. For instance, why do bad things happen to good people? Why does an innocent newborn baby struggle for her very existence, while a murderer goes free? Why does God take a seven-year-old child to heaven and leave a grouchy old man to make all those around him miserable? Many have asked similar questions. I do not think there is a good human answer. Consider what Isaiah wrote. "'My thoughts are nothing like your thoughts,' says the Lord, 'And my ways are far beyond anything you could imagine'" Isaiah 55:8-9 (NLT).

Many of us have stumbled because of these verses and the life situations that we face. What we know is what God tells us. For you created my inmost being; you knit me together in my mother's womb. I praise you because I am fearfully and wonderfully made" Psalm 139:13,14 (NIV).

He alone knows our purpose and our life span. He has a far greater plan for our lives than we can imagine. In God's eternity, our lifetime here on earth is just like a "blink of an eye," yet He cares about every second of every minute that we live here on earth. He has a divine plan for each one of us. How important we are to Him! "But You, O Lord, are a God of compassion and mercy, slow to get angry and filled with unfailing love and faithfulness" Psalm 86:15 (NLT).

Personal Note:

I used to be afraid to question God. I thought that if I questioned Him, He would be unhappy with me, but He does not expect me to understand His ways. Questions can bring about an intimacy with Him that can move me to a completely new level of comprehension of my Father and what He is like.

Even when I do not understand something, He is faithful to give me peace and comfort through my trial when I call upon Him. Even when something is so big and difficult that I am very overwhelmed, if I let Him, He just picks me up, wraps His arms around me, and holds me secure in His love until the storm passes by.

Prayer:

Oh, Father, I don't always understand Your ways, but I know that you have a plan in everything You do. My time here on earth may be full of trials and doubts but thank you for keeping me in the shelter of Your love as I go through the valleys. In Jesus' name, Amen.

Your Reflections:

Day 9

God is . . . Always Accessible

Bible Reading: Hebrews 4:12-16

I remember an old song I sang with the words, "Operator, Get Me Jesus on the Line." It was a fun song to sing, but the whole premise was wrong, because we don't have to go through an operator. Jesus *is* the Operator! We have clear access to the Father through Jesus Christ His Son. Paul wrote in Hebrews, "Therefore, He is able once and forever to save those who come to God through Him. He lives forever to intercede with God on their behalf" Hebrews 7:25 (NLT).

Jesus paid the price so that we could not only be saved from our sin, but so that we could have communication with the Father through Him! This is all part of God's grace for us. He has always desired to have conversation with us, but our sin got in the way.

None of us is free from sin. We are tainted until we come to Christ through His sacrifice. We think of our Savior often for our salvation, but He is so much more! Because of Jesus' willingness to pay the price for us on the cross, we have freedom to be intimate with the Father! When we try to imagine this, it is astounding!

My Creator who holds the universe in place, who controls my very existence, wants to have a conversation with me. I have always thought it was fabulous that I could write to the White House and they would send a note of congratulations to someone in our family when they turned eighty years old. We did that for our parents on both sides and received a form letter. However, our God wants to get "up close and personal" with us. We read in I John 3:1 "See how very much our Father loves us, for He calls us His children, and that is what we are!" (NLT). To truly comprehend this is mind-boggling!

Personal Note:

From my journal on January 4, 2000: "Sometimes I feel so alone and I forget that God is always there for me. He is just waiting for me to talk to Him. As I have grown in Him, I have discovered that I can indeed have an intimacy with Him and He is very real."

The words of "In the Garden"[2] are a wonderful example of how God re-addresses His desire to be intimate with me.

> *And He walks with me*
> *and He talks with me,*
> *And He tells me I am His own*
> *And the joy we share as we tarry there,*
> *None other, has ever known.*
> *Words and music by C. Austin Mills*

How often I have sung this old hymn! It tells of an intimacy that is within my grasp. He is my Father! He longs to commune with all His children! I am so glad that I am learning to invite Him more and more to fellowship with me. He is just waiting for that invitation!

Prayer:

Oh Father, I thank You and praise You that I have access to Your throne through my Lord and Savior Jesus Christ. I pray that You will continue Your work in me. May I open my heart and really listen for Your direction as I begin to understand Your ways. In Jesus' name, Amen.

Your Reflections:

Day 10

God is . . . The Scepter of Justice

Bible Reading: Esther 5:1-7

For many of us, the Book of Esther is one of the beloved love stories in the Bible. It is the most well known example of the use of a scepter that we have. "All the king's servants and the people of the king's provinces, know that any man or woman who goes into the inner court of the king who has not been called, he has but one law: Put all to death except the one to whom the king holds out the golden scepter, that he may live" Esther 4:11-12a (NKJ).

Esther knew this law and yet her mission was so important that she was willing to risk her life to talk to the king. The king held out the golden scepter to her and God used her in a mighty way to save His people.

God has a scepter also. It is a scepter of justice. He will hold it out to everyone who has been clothed in the righteousness of His Son's sacrifice on the cross. The psalmist wrote, "Your throne, O God, endures for ever and ever; You rule with a scepter of justice. You love justice and hate evil. Therefore God, your God, has anointed you, pouring out the oil of joy on You, more than on anyone else" Psalm 45:6-7 (NLT). His love far surpasses our understanding.

He will fill each of us with His joy! What a wonderful gift! "Commit everything you do to the Lord. Trust Him, and He will help you. He will make your innocence radiate like the dawn and the justice of your cause will shine like the noonday sun!" Psalm 37:5-6 (NLT). We who love Him will never have to fear His justice. His Son has already paid for our access to Him and with radiant joy; we will walk confidently toward Him. He will hold out His scepter to us, and we will be ushered into His eternal family.

Personal Note:

Recently I saw a wonderful movie about Queen Esther. I remember the scene of Esther opening the doors of the King's banquet hall and entering without His permission. As she walked toward him, everyone was silent and watching as finally the king held out his scepter to her.

I think of God's righteousness covering me because of Jesus' sacrifice on the cross. I will walk the beautiful corridor toward my King and as He holds out His scepter for me to enter, Jesus will be there sitting next to Him. Heaven will rejoice, God will fill me with His joy, and another child will enter the kingdom of God forever and ever. I can hardly wait!

Prayer:

Thank You, my Father, for the unspeakable gift of Your Son that I might be a child in Your kingdom. You have so many things awaiting me. I cannot even dream of the riches and beauty that You have prepared for me. I praise You for Your abundant love and grace. In Jesus' name, Amen.

Your Reflections:

Day 11

God is . . . Majestic

Bible Reading: Psalm 8:1-9

Majestic! What a powerful word! When I think of majesty, kings and kingdoms come to mind. I have never been inside a palace or even seen a real castle in person; but if I were to visit Europe, I would see the splendor of castles dotting the landscape.

Webster's defines majestic as "sovereign, power, authority, splendor, grandeur." What a wonderful description of our Heavenly Father. Even though we have seen some of the magnificence of royal weddings and other events, we only have a glimpse of what majesty is really all about.

A few countries still have royalty and I am sure that their palaces are very spectacular. The most commonly known, for most of us, is England. I will never forget the elegance and splendor of Princess Diana going down that long aisle to give her hand in marriage to Prince Charles, the heir to that throne. We saw royalty in all of its pomp and circumstance; and many of us were glued to our television screens just seeing this fairy-tale event.

God's majesty is so far above anything we might imagine that it is almost unbelievable to us. It just spills over into all of nature as well. I think of an eagle soaring high in the sky—its regal beauty revealing the freedom and power displayed in its mighty wings. I see the elegance and beauty of all creation as I travel through brilliant landscapes. What a fantastic view it is for me to see the grandeur of God's creation as I approach an enormous snow-capped mountain.

Living in Oregon, I am blessed to see the beautiful splendor of five of these mountains without going far from home. How gorgeous they are as the sun sends its rays to bring into focus the brilliance of the glacial snow adorning the tops of these wonderful works of our Creator.

However, the most majestic thing of all was written by the psalmist. "O LORD, our Lord how majestic is Your name in all the earth! You have set Your glory above the heavens; from the lips of children and infants You have ordained praise." He goes on to tell of the magnificence of all God has created. He then ends this fabulous psalm of praise the same way he started it. "O LORD, our Lord, how majestic is Your name in all the earth" Psalm 8:1,9 (NIV).

Personal Note:

God's majesty is so incredible! I think that most of the books of the Old Testament tell of His royalty and power as we go through His genealogy of the human race and its history. God's chosen ones had phenomenal things happen to them as they learned to walk in His ways. He is still the same almighty God today! His greatness brings me to my knees in worship of His glory and splendor. I look forward to being more amazed by His grandeur as I learn to walk ever closer to this royal and regal Father who rules and reigns in all His sovereignty and authority. "His majesty, the King of the Universe!" My Father and my God!

Prayer:

My Father, truly You are an awesome God! Your magnificence and glory are so great that I can only get a glimpse of who You are and what You have for me. I bow humbly at Your feet. Thank You for including me in this powerful kingdom through Jesus Christ my Lord. In His name, Amen.

Your Reflections:

Day 12

God is . . . The Almighty, El-Shaddai

Bible Reading: Genesis 17:1-16

Who is this amazing God who reveals Himself in such dramatic fashion to those whose hearts are open and ready to accept His ways? When I kneel before God Almighty in reverence and awe and concentrate on His holiness, it transforms me and begins to shape my life into the life that He has for me.

Moses wrote, "When Abram was ninety-nine years old, the LORD appeared to him and said: "I am El-Shaddai, God Almighty. Serve me faithfully and live a blameless life and I will make a covenant with you, by which I will guarantee to give you countless descendants" Genesis 17:1-2 (NLT). God further explained to him that He would confirm His covenant with Abram and all His descendants after him. During this meeting with him, God changed Abram's name to Abraham, which means "the father of many nations."

This is the first reference to God Almighty! God revealed this name about Himself and that name affected Abraham's life from that day to this. God kept His promise to Abraham. Throughout all generations, his seed has flourished around the world. El-Shaddai totally changed Abraham's life.

"O Lord God Almighty, who is like You? You are mighty, O Lord and Your faithfulness surrounds You" Psalm 89:8 (NIV). I am in total awe of this mighty and faithful God of the universe who cares so much about a tiny dot that He created and purposed to live in this very time and place in history. Yes, the Almighty El-Shaddai has changed my life and I know that this is just the beginning! I will never be the same since I met the Almighty El-Shaddai!

Personal Note:

This has been the most precious and yet the hardest writing thus far. To put down on paper my thoughts about God Almighty and what He has done in my life brings so much joy that it brings tears to my eyes, making it hard to write. His holiness is so awesome, His mercy so great that my heart is lifted in praise to His almightiness. If you have not had the experience of facing God's greatness and sovereignty, keep praying; it is there for all of us. We just need to give Him an open heart. He is an amazing God! He has brought me to places I could never even dream!

Prayer:

Father, I bow before You right now in reverence of who You are. I am thankful that through Your Son, Jesus Christ, I can come to You and start to know just how almighty and powerful You are. Make me worthy of the reality that You are my El-Shaddai, the Almighty God! I thank You in Jesus' name, Amen.

Your Reflections:

Day 13

God is . . . Our Covenant Keeper

Bible Reading: Exodus 6:1-8

God always uses whoever can get the job done. Sometimes willingly and sometimes with much anguish, however, His plan will be carried out by someone. God showed Himself to Abraham and made a lasting covenant with him that he would be the father of many nations. We see in Genesis how God kept that covenant to included Isaac, Abraham's son, and then continued it to include his grandson Jacob. From then on, whenever the covenant was mentioned, it always read, "The God of Abraham, Isaac and Jacob."

God changed Jacob's name to Israel, during a night of wrestling with a messenger sent from God. When morning came, Jacob would not let the man go until He blessed him. "Then the man said, your name will no longer be Jacob, but Israel, because you have struggled with God and with men and have overcome" Genesis 32:28 (NIV).

God was true to His word. Jacob had twelve sons and they eventually became the twelve tribes of Israel. They grew to be so large in number within the land of Egypt that the Pharaoh at the time made them slaves. That was when God intervened again. "And God said to Moses, I am Yahweh the Lord. I appeared to Abraham, to Isaac, and to Jacob as El-Shaddai, God Almighty, but I did not reveal my name, Yahweh, to them" Exodus 6:2,3 (NLT). God had another miracle man to use. Moses felt very inadequate, but He was God's man . . . and the rest is history!

Personal Note:

I will never know what great plans God may have for me until I yield myself totally to His will and let Him use me.

As I am learning more about Him, I have a sense of wonderment around me. I am so completely awed by my magnificent God. How unworthy I feel. How inadequate. However, that is all right because I don't have to be adequate. He told Paul, "My grace is all you need. My power works best in weakness" 2 Corinthians 12:9a (NLT). God is a covenant keeper! I am so glad that He loves to use anyone who comes humbly before Him with his or her inabilities. He takes my weakness and it becomes an incredible force that He can change and use by His mighty hand. I only have to be willing to yield it all to Him.

Prayer:

Father, I know that You have a great plan to keep Your covenant with Your chosen ones. Thank you that because of the blood of Jesus we are all included in the new covenant. I pray that You will help me to allow You to work Your will in my life. Use me for Your glory! In Jesus' name, Amen.

Your Reflections:

Day 14

God is . . . A Promise Keeper

Bible Reading: 2 Samuel 7:8-17

David was a warrior. He had spent most of his life fighting enemies. King Saul hated him and tried to take his life on numerous occasions, but God was always with him. David had the kind of heart that God could use.

After most of the fighting was over and they were living in a more peaceful time, David looked around him and saw his gorgeous home; but God still lived in a tent. He wanted to build the most beautiful home he could imagine to worship God. That was when God made His third covenant with Israel. Through Nathan the prophet God told David, "no!" That would not be for him to do, but God then honored David with a far greater blessing. "Tell David that your house and your kingdom will continue before Me for all time and your throne will be secure forever" 2 Samuel 7:16 (NLT).

David was so humbled by this. We read this beautiful prayer of gratitude from King David to God. "O Lord of Heaven's Armies, God of Israel, I have been bold enough to pray this prayer to You because You have revealed all this to Your servant saying, 'I will build a house for you, a dynasty of kings!' For You are God, O Sovereign Lord. Your words are truth and You have promised these good things to your servant. And now, may it please You to bless the house of Your servant, so that it may continue forever before You. For You have spoken, and when You grant a blessing to your servant, O Sovereign Lord, it is an eternal blessing!" 2 Samuel 7:27-29 (NLT). As we know, Jesus came through the lineage of David. Through Christ, God's kingdom will be established forever and ever. When God makes a promise to us, He will never go back on His word. What a promise keeper!

Personal Note:

God always keeps His promises. Sometimes I need to take a walk back in history to see how He works in such a beautiful way. Through His Word, I see how first the covenant was given to Abraham to multiply His seed as the stars in the sky and the sand on the earth. My, how He has done that! Then through Moses He promised that His people would have an inheritance of land forever. In 1948, after centuries of wandering, God gave Israel back its land. Through King David God established His kingdom forever! We still can look forward to the fulfillment of that promise.

When Christ returns to earth, Israel will finally have a lasting peace. Jesus will set up His kingdom for a millennium and we who have believed and received Christ as our Savior, along with those redeemed in Israel, will never know war or violence again! The Prince of Peace will have come back to fulfill the final promise.

When I look at the turmoil around me, it is hard to think this can happen, but God's perfect plan will be accomplished! He will fulfill His promise! He is a promise keeper! I can count on that!

Prayer:

My precious Father, Your promises will never fail! You are trustworthy. You hold my future in Your hands. Thank You that I need not worry about the unrest around me when I allow You to guide my life. In Your Son's powerful name, Jesus!, Amen.

Your Reflections:

Day 15

God is . . . Transcendent

Bible Reading: Psalm 33:13-17, 93:1-5

There is much around us that point to God's magnificence. We know that He is almighty and that He is exalted beyond our understanding. He is righteous and holy, watches over the universe, and keeps everything in total order. He is beyond anything that we can imagine. When we look at nature, however, we begin to understand a little better about this transcendent God. When we are at the seashore, we see His power and might in the crashing of the waves against the rocks, the brilliance of the sands as the waves gently enfold them and carry them out to sea. Far above our heads we watch the strength and beauty of an eagle soaring over the cliffs and up into the clouds.

When we are in the mountains, we see the splendor and vastness of the majestic mountains and the depths of the green and verdant valleys, the beauty and delicacy of the tiniest flowers. We see how much He loves color when we look at a peacock with its amazing array of vivid beauty, or an intricate butterfly floating through the air—a velvety soft flower growing in the crevice of a rock.

Yet Isaiah wrote, "The grass withers and the flowers fall because the breath of the Lord blows on them; surely the people are grass. The grass withers, the flowers fall, but the word of our God stands forever" Isaiah 40:7-8 (NIV). We are like a blade of grass compared to Him, yet He loves us with an everlasting love. He wants us to revere Him, to worship and praise Him! Can we even begin to understand the kind of love He has for us that transcends beyond our wildest imaginings?

David wrote many psalms that speak to God's transcendence and unfailing love. These verses speak to that. "But the Lord watches over those who fear Him, those who rely on His unfailing love . . . Let

47

Your unfailing love surround us, Lord, for our hope is in You alone"
Psalm 33:18,22 (NLT).

Personal Note:

*He created me to love and commune with Him, but also to remember that He is
God! He is not just a benevolent father who pats me on the head or disciplines
me whenever I sin, but He wants me to always remember that He is exalted way
above my comprehension, transcendent in all of His glory!*

*I am like a fleck of lint on a black dress. I would flick it away without the least
bit of thought or feeling of guilt. But God? He would carefully lift it off the
dress and carry it gently and lovingly in His mighty fingers, breathe into it the
breath of life, give it a free will and then make a home for it to live with Him
forever. Now that is a God beyond my understanding. Transcendent in His
righteousness and might, yet loving to the utmost heights.*

Prayer:

**My Father, I am just starting to get a glimpse of whom and what You
are. How I honor You. I worship and praise You with all of my heart.
You are so far above everything, yet You love me with an everlasting
love. How I thank You for that! In Jesus' glorious name, Amen.**

Your Reflections:

Day 16

God is . . . Multi-faceted

Bible Reading: Isaiah 57:14-21

I remember fondly the night Don asked me to marry him. When he proposed, he slipped a diamond ring on my finger. It exploded with color in the streetlight in front of my home. I thought it was the most beautiful thing I had ever seen. The ring was too large for my finger, but I wanted to wear it and show my family before we had it sized. With eyes shining, I ran into the house to show my mother; however, she was already in bed and asleep. I went to sleep with my fist clenched tightly around that gorgeous multi-faceted ring on my finger.

The next morning the first thing I wanted to see was that diamond! It was gone! I searched the bed, under the bed, and all around the room. I cried hysterically as my mother gently tried to comfort me. I finally found it in a crease in the blanket. Oh, how gorgeous it was! It had so many colors that it was beyond description. It stood alone in its beauty.

God is so far above even the most valuable diamond in the world. He has so many facets that we cannot even describe Him in one quality or even three hundred sixty five of them! His voice alone is beyond description. Job wrote, "God's voice is glorious in the thunder. We cannot even imagine the greatness of His power" Job 37:5 (NLT). The wonder and beauty of our marvelous God is beyond description.

On the one hand, we have a God who rules and reigns from far above the heavenly places. He is powerful, yet gentle to anyone who loves Him. He brings severe judgment on the wicked, but shelters us in the shadow of His wings when we are hurting. He is holy, but merciful. He created the earth, but can destroy it with a word.

Nations rise and fall by His word. Kingdoms crumble at His command. He hates wickedness, but dearly loves those who call upon His name. "Call to me and I will answer you and tell you great and unsearchable things you do not know" Jeremiah 33:3 (NIV). To begin to know this multi-faceted God brings so much joy that my diamond ring pales in comparison! How magnificent He is!

Personal Note:

I am only beginning to understand a little of how brilliant and glorious God is! His beauty is beyond words. His unfailing love and mercy are beyond description. How I love to worship Him! My favorite song has always been "His Eye is On the Sparrow." It is just incomprehensible to me how such a multi-faceted God, who looks down on me as a blade of grass, could love me enough to know everything about me, and even more, care about me.

Nevertheless, His eye is on the lowly sparrow; so I have no doubt that He watches over and cares for me. Yet "The Lord merely spoke and the heavens were created. He breathed the word, and all the stars were born" Psalm 33:6. (NLT). Is it any wonder that my heart overflows with worship and praise to this all-encompassing God who wants me to call Him, "my Father?"

Prayer:

Oh Father, You are so far beyond my understanding. So unequally diverse that I cannot even begin to comprehend You. Your beauty is beyond description. How very grateful I am for Your unfailing love. In Jesus' matchless name, Amen.

Your Reflections:

Day 17

God is . . . Exalted

Bible Reading: Psalm 89:5-16

When I was growing up, children were taught to respect those who were older. We learned to call adults Mr., Mrs., or Miss. We were taught to respect our President because of His office, whether or not we agreed with his politics. We don't really use any titles anymore and many times, we scorn those in authority rather than respect them.

There are many Scriptures that could be used to describe our God who is exalted above all else. However, I love this passage and the way the New Living Translation words it, because it is so descriptive of many of the attributes of our exalted God: "For who in all of heaven can compare with the Lord? What mightiest angel is anything like the Lord? The highest angelic powers stand in awe of God. He is far more awesome than all who surround His throne" Psalm 89:6-7. Now that is exalted!

These are the beautiful beings that are "up close and personal" with God every day forever and ever. Yet they reverence Him above all. Nonetheless, many people dare to shake their fists at God and say, "If there was a God, why would He let this happen?" There are even those mortals who deny that He even exists at all.

As Christians, we at times go about our daily business barely acknowledging His existence, but when we get into trouble, we turn quickly to Him. We get so busy living life that we forget the One who gave us that life. I must confess I have been guilty of this myself at times. Perhaps it is that many of us do not understand how to exalt Him. We barely understand the concept of the word "respect."

Exaltation is far above respect. To exalt Him means that I hold Him in the highest esteem. It is a reverent awe. It is how our heavenly Father wants us to praise and worship Him. David tells us how to do that. "Blessed are those who have learned to acclaim You, who walk in the light of Your presence, O Lord. They rejoice in Your name all day long; they exult in Your righteousness" Psalm 89:15-16 (NIV). Yes, that is exaltation! That is how we respect our God!

Personal Note:

Getting to know my Father more personally has been a fabulous "ride" so far. I cannot even fathom what else He has in store for me as I become more in tune to His will in my life. I am so overwhelmed by His majesty and love that it is hard for me to contain, let alone put on paper. I guess, though, that if the most powerful angels in heaven are awed by Him, it is no wonder that I am overcome with the grandeur of my Creator. The best part is, because of Christ's sacrifice, I can call this magnificent Lord, "my Father."

Prayer:

Father, oh how I love to call You that, my Creator and my God. I exalt You, and proclaim Your goodness and might. I worship and adore You. Continue working in my life as I become more familiar and intimate with You, because of Christ, Amen.

Your Reflections:

Day 18

God is . . . The Immortal Name

Bible Reading: Genesis 1:1-8

What is in a name? Names are very interesting and can be very informative. Many times when we are expecting a child, we can anguish over what name to choose. Often it takes until the baby is born and even then, we are still pondering the best name while we sign the birth certificate.

Nevertheless, when that child is born and the decision is made, it is the ideal name and fits perfectly. There are times that we name a baby specifically because there is significance in the name we chose. Whenever we write something whether it is a book or even a check, we have our signature or name on it. That name stays with us for the rest of our life and we are known by it.

The Bible is clear about who its author is as well. Although the name is not on the outside of the book, we only have to go four words into the first chapter of Genesis to find out the author. "In the beginning GOD!" Twenty-nine times in the first chapter alone God mentioned who He is.

The Hebrew for this very first name is *Elohim* and it is in the plural form. Our Triune Immortal God makes it very plain who He is! In Genesis 1:26 God states, "Let Us make man in Our image, in Our likeness" (NIV). Therefore, we were made in body, soul and spirit! He was there before anything existed and will be there forever and ever!

Personal Note:

As humans, we are the only ones in all of creation that God made in His likeness. He created everything that exists, from the highest angel to the lowliest insect. Yet in all of creation, there is nothing like us. He created us in His image so that we could live with Him eternally. Our mortal bodies will be changed to immortality in His forever world.

For now though, we are mortal. His desire is to have an intimate relationship with us while we live here on earth—one where we will love Him with all of our hearts. However, along with that He has given us a free will. In that one act, He showed the greatest love possible, the freedom to choose Him or reject Him.

I am so glad that He chose me; and I in turn chose Him. That choice is what makes me different from everything else in creation. That choice led Adam and Eve to sin, and Christ to have to die for us. That was the only way that I could be redeemed from sin and again be made whole through Him. Christ's choice allowed me to become part of God's family and gave me access to the Father. God is immortal and because of Christ's victory over death, I have been made to live eternally with Him! How I praise Him for that!

Prayer:

My God and my Father, thank You for creating me in Your image. I praise and honor You because You want a real relationship with me. How I revere You, who by a word can speak anything into existence. I praise Your everlasting name and I exalt You anew in my life, from this day forward. In Jesus' name, Amen.

Your Reflections:

Day 19

God is . . . In the Stillness

Bible Reading: Psalm 23:1-6

When I think of stillness, I think of the twenty-third Psalm. It probably is the most beloved of all the psalms. We hear it often at memorial services and quoted to someone when they are very ill. In it, I not only find solace in my Shepherd, but it brings me insight into God the Father, Jehovah-Shalom. My God of Peace. When I need God's stillness, I meditate on this psalm. He wants me to have a special quiet time where He can restore my spirit and I can allow my mind to rest in Him.

When we bought this house, I knew that this was my home of peace. I walked into the living room overlooking our wooded yard and it was so restful! Now it is my special room where I have quiet time with my Father.

Waiting, stillness, quiet! What a challenge this has been for me. My whole life I have been busy scurrying about, but it was not until about a year and one half ago that I really started resting and trusting in quietness.

Isaiah wrote, "In repentance and rest is your salvation, in quietness and trust is your strength, but you would have none of it." Isaiah continues, "Yet the Lord longs to be gracious to you; He rises to show you compassion. For the Lord is a God of justice. Blessed are all who wait for Him!" Isaiah 30:15,18 (NIV).

Even when I am in my busy mode, I am learning stillness in the midst of activity, as I trust God's control in my life. I can find rest for my soul even when everything around me is stressful. It always depends on my willingness to allow God into the quietness of my soul, though difficulties surround me. The Psalmist wrote, "Turn away from evil and do good. Search for peace, and work to maintain it" Psalm 34:14 (NLT). Yes, in the midst of everyday stress, I can search for peace; and sometimes it does take a lot of work for me to maintain it. Nonetheless, God will bring me closer to His stillness when I search for Him with all of my heart.

Personal Note:

From my journal on February 24, 2000: I wrote about peace: "Oh Lord, how I needed this devotional today. For several months, I have been searching for a way to quiet myself and meditate on You. I simply have not known how to do this. As I learn more about who You are, I realize that I must get to know you in a much deeper way so that my thoughts are in tune with Your thoughts."

I wrote this while I was temporarily living in an apartment next door to my husband and father-in-law. We had moved Dad into a unit in our triplex knowing that Don would need to live with his father. Dad's health had deteriorated and we felt that it was not safe for him to live alone. The next year, we bought this house. I call it my home of "peace." How grateful I am that my heavenly Father answered my prayer so completely!

Prayer:

Father, teach me to seek You and calm my heart and mind so that I can hear You more clearly. I love You and thank you for the stillness of Your presence, for Your compassion, Your mercy and Your grace. In Jesus' name, Amen.

Your Reflections:

Day 20

God is . . . Worthy of Reverence

Bible Reading: Hebrews 5: 7-10

When I come before my heavenly Father, I need to come in reverence and awe. As I learn to be still before God, I also learn that I need to approach Him with honor and respect. There is great power in the humility that ushers me into the midst of His holiness and brings my spirit into a reverent attitude to worship Him.

I am learning that when I first come to Him in prayer, just calling Him "Father" cultivates a deep respect. Jesus taught this. He was asked how we should pray. He said, '"Pray like this, 'Our Father in heaven, may Your name be kept holy"' Matthew 6-9 (NLT). Now that is reverence and awe! There was no one who esteemed the Father more than Jesus.

Hebrews tells us that, "During the days of Jesus' life on earth, He offered up prayers and petitions with loud cries and tears, to the One who could save Him from death, and He was heard, because of His reverent submission" Hebrews 5:7 (NIV).

If Christ came to His Father showing such high esteem, how much more should we? What better example than His! "Reverent submission"—I like that. I think there is a time for casually talking to God. I do it all the time as I am working, driving, or shopping,—no matter where I may be, There is a very short verse in the Bible that has always been with me. It is just three words. The New Living Translation reads, "Never stop praying" 1 Thessalonians 5:17. It means that at any given moment my spirit can be ready to pray. However, when I really want to communicate with my Father, I have a special place and I come with a reverent attitude toward Him.

Personal Note:

From my journal on February 24, 2000: "It is so important to worship God. If I do not have a clear picture of who He is, then it is very difficult for me to worship Him. This has been the problem in my quest to learn to meditate on Him. I would try, but since I did not have a clear picture of who He is, my thoughts were scattered and I was unable to concentrate.

My Father has taught me a lot since then. I try to start my prayer with respect and praise. I quiet my spirit with thanksgiving and worship for a time before I bring any requests to Him. I want my first words spoken in prayer to be "all about Him." I look forward to my praise and worship time with Him and as I do this more often, my love and faith grow. He has blessed me in so many ways.

Coming to Him in humility and worship is one of the ways God allowed me to grow and learn from Him. He took the devotional I was reading and permitted me to long for a deeper understanding Of Him. That was how this work was birthed. What a wonderful God and Father and how I am awestruck by Him!

Prayer:

Father, I come to You in admiration and awe as I realize how holy and pure You are. I praise You because You are exalted above all else, and I thank You because You also reach down and pick me up in Your arms and cherish me. You have made me to be exactly who I am. Thank You for such great love, in Jesus' name, Amen.

Your Reflections:

Day 21

God is . . . Creator of the Universe

Bible Reading: Psalm 104:1-9

Recently I watched a wonderful program on television that I try to view whenever I am available called "Creation in the 21st Century." It begins with a sky so full of stars dotting the universe that they are impossible to count. I cannot even comprehend the vastness and magnitude of that.

The magnificence of our world alone is overwhelming. Psalm 104 is a beautiful picture of the days of creation described in Genesis. It gives me a poetic view of each day of creation as it unfolds. "Let all that I am praise the Lord. O Lord my God, how great You are! You are robed with honor and majesty. You are dressed in a robe of light. You stretch out the starry curtain of the heavens; You lay out the rafters of Your home in the rain clouds. You make the clouds Your chariot; You ride upon the wings of the wind. The winds are Your messengers; flames of fire are Your servants. You placed the world on its foundations so it would never be moved" Psalm 104:1-5 (NLT).

As wonderful as this description is of God creating our world, we need to remember that our planet and our galaxy are mere specks on God's telescope of the entire universe. The Psalmist wrote, "When I consider Your heavens, the works of Your fingers, the moon and the stars, which You have set in place, what is man that You are mindful of him, the son of man that You care for him?" Psalm 8:3-4 (NIV).

If our world is only a tiny dot on God's telescope, try to imagine how small and insignificant we are. Yet He cares for every detail of our planet. More importantly, He cares for each of us, personally. He took dust and formed us in all our complexity and He created us in His image yet each unique in our own way. With our modern technology, we can determine this difference, because we now can read the DNA of everyone and each of us has a different DNA. Solomon wrote, "As you do not know the path of the wind, or how the body was formed in a mother's womb, so you cannot understand the work of God, the Maker of all things" Ecclesiastes 11:5 (NIV).

Personal Note:

It is way beyond my understanding to comprehend a God who can form the extensive universe and yet cares so much for me! That is why I must rely on faith. Paul wrote in Hebrews, "By faith we understand that the entire universe was formed at God's command, that what we now see did not come from anything that was seen" Hebrews 11:3 (NLT). Only through faith can I even begin to grasp a little of this indescribable Maker of the universe. How magnificent it is to realize the depth of His love for me!

Prayer:

Father, You truly are way beyond my comprehension, yet You reach down and touch my life in such an astonishing way. Your wonders are far above anything that I can imagine. I thank You that You, who created the entire universe, created me in Your image. I magnify Your matchless name. Amen.

Your Reflections:

Day 22

God is . . . Poured Out

Bible Reading: Joel 2:28-32

I picture this description of God in Joel chapter two, as an endless resource of anything and everything I could possibly want. We are the empty vessel. He is just waiting for us to take the cap off and let Him fill us. In our passage in Joel, he talks about how God will pour out His spirit on all flesh! This is talking about the last days before Christ comes to earth to reign. However, I also think that God loves individual empty vessels that He can fill.

We often hear the expression about optimists and pessimists. The optimist's glass is always half-full while the pessimist's glass is always half-empty. God's vessels are always overflowing, as there is no going half way with Him!

He loves to pour out His blessings and abundance upon us and our children. "For I will pour water on the thirsty land and streams on the dry ground. I will pour out my Spirit on your offspring and my blessing on your descendants" Isaiah 44:3 (NIV).

God also loves to pour out His blessing on those who tithe. The familiar passage in Malachi reminds us, "'Bring all the tithes into the storehouse so there will be enough food in my Temple. If you do' says the Lord of Heaven's Armies, 'I will open the window of heaven for you. I will pour out a blessing so great you will not have enough room to take it in! Try it! Put Me to the test!'" Malachi 3:10 (NLT). God's joy is sending us a deluge of His blessing when we let Him. When He does, there is nothing like it—abundant blessing! That is our God!

Personal Note:

What a great promise from God! Because our Father is a God of covenant, if I give Him my tithe with a willing heart, He wants to drench me with all kinds of favor. He will open the windows of heaven and pour out His prosperity on me! When I try to imagine what is behind that window in heaven, I cannot even fathom the riches and blessing He has in store for me. However, He is looking for a willing heart: one that is just waiting for Him to continually pour His love, joy, peace, provision, contentment and so much more. He will not withhold anything from me if I am responsive and open to trust Him fully and freely.

Prayer:

Oh Father, You want to shower me with everything good and pure according to Your purpose in my life. Lord, help me to empty myself of anything that will get in the way of Your very best for me. In Jesus' name, Amen.

Your Reflections:

Day 23

God is . . . "The Bottom Line"

Bible Reading: Psalm 73:12-17

My husband, Don, has been a business consultant for many years. On his business card is written, "Better your bottom line" and he has helped many in business to do just that. While we are here on earth, we want to be as profitable as possible so that we can support our families and give them a secure future.

We may look around us, and see people who have no regard at all for God. Among them are often the most successful and prosperous. They seem to have everything while we are struggling to make "ends meet." It is tempting to look up to God and ask, "Why? Why does this life have to be so hard?" Psalm 73 is a psalm of Asaph. Apparently, he understood those feelings because he wrote, "But as for me, my feet had almost slipped; I had nearly lost my foothold. For I envied the arrogant when I saw the prosperity of the wicked. They have no struggles; their bodies are healthy and strong. They are free from the burdens common to man; they are not plagued by human ills" Psalm 73:2-5 (NIV).

It is so easy to feel just like Asaph. By the end of this psalm, he has His "bottom line" well established. "Those who are far from You will perish; You destroy all who are unfaithful to You. As for me, it is good to be near God. I have made the Sovereign Lord my refuge, I will tell of all Your deeds" Psalm 73:27-28 (NIV).

Personal Note:

The bottom line is this that no matter how much I have or do not have materially, this life is not my final destination. My focus and security come from God. No matter what line I set, God will always be above it. When I place expectations on Him, I have already lost the battle. God loves to give me more than I could imagine, but when I expect Him to do so, I have already closed the window of heaven. A simple little chorus that we sang when I was young went something like this:

> *"The windows of heaven are opened,*
> *the blessings are falling tonight,*
> *And there's joy, joy, joy in my heart,*
> *for Jesus made everything right.*
> *I gave Him my old tattered garment.*
> *He gave me a robe of pure white*
> *I'm feasting today on that manna from heaven*
> *and that's why I'm happy tonight*

Simplistic, yes, but it is the bottom line!

Prayer:

Father, thank You that You supply all my needs. Forgive me for doubting Your provision for me. I know that my riches are in Your kingdom and whatever You provide for me down here is frosting on the cake! I praise You with all of my heart. In Jesus' name, Amen.

Your Reflections:

Day 24

God is . . . Truth

Bible Reading: John 8:34-47

What is truth? It is hard to know at times. Many learn to stretch the truth when they are very young. We often call these "little white lies." We might tell them, because we do not want to hurt someone's feelings, or maybe it will get us out of a tight spot or it may seem easier than trying to explain the truth.

Pilate once asked Jesus, "What is truth?" Truth is God and God is truth! God by His very nature is accurate in all He does. He sent His Son into the world and as we read the Gospels, we find Jesus saying repeatedly, "I tell you the truth." This has become one of the precious phrases I love reading in Scripture.

Just as God is fidelity, it is equally true that Satan cannot tell the truth. Jesus declares the real difference between Himself, and the devil. Our Lord does not mince words when He says, "You belong to your father, the devil, and you want to carry out your father's desires. He was a murderer from the beginning, not holding to the truth, for there is no truth in him. When he lies, he speaks his native language, for he is a liar and the father of lies" John 8:44 (NIV).

Jesus spoke plainly when He was dealing with anyone, friend or foe. He often put the Pharisees in their place. He also told Peter, "Get behind me, Satan" when he was out of line. He always told it plainly and directly! Because He is trustworthy, He will not sugarcoat things nor will He lie.

Jesus spoke so much about authenticity because that was His very nature from the beginning. John wrote, "God is a spirit and they that worship Him must worship Him in spirit and in truth!" John 4:24. (KJV). Others may lie, but God is truth!

Personal Note:

To be truthful is to experience real freedom. Jesus said in John 8:32, "You will know the truth and the truth will set you free!" (NLT), There is nothing more liberating than truthfulness. How He loves it when we tell the truth. He hates lying because all lying is from Satan. Truthfulness comes from God!

When I was a little girl, my grandmother told me that a lie is anything that is intended to deceive. She was absolutely right! I have not always abided by that, however. I wish I could say that I had, but I would have to plead guilty before my Father's throne. It is my heart's desire, as I grow in Him, to be honest and truthful; and when I do err, I will come before Him and ask for His forgiveness; because I have learned that no matter how much I might try to sugarcoat something, there really is no such thing as a white lie!

Prayer:

Father, I come before You as I search my own heart. You know that the heart is deceitful and desperately wicked; but I know that I may come before You in truth, with a clean heart, one You have cleansed by Your grace and mercy. Thank You for Your steadfastness. In Jesus' name, Amen.

Your Reflections:

Day 25

God is . . . Just

Bible Reading: Deuteronomy 32:1-4

God is not only true He is also just. Everything He does is fair. Trying to explain this to a grieving mother who has just lost a child, or a child racked with cancer at an early age, is not in our power to do. The only comfort that we can give someone in these times is our prayer support and the hollow words that echo even in our own ears. We feel so helpless.

Believing that God is just is probably one of the most difficult lessons we all have to face. We see injustice all around us; and sometimes we absolutely do not understand God's will in a situation. We cannot seem to grasp God's plan, because it is beyond us.

This is a hard thing for us to understand, because we try to judge God by our human standards. We need to remember the bottom line of who He is. God is just because He can be nothing else. He knows the complete picture of the entire universe, as well as the future of everyone on the planet.

His justice and righteousness take in everything! That is when we can be near to God if we reach out to Him. We are always at a crossroad with two choices. Solomon wrote, "A wise person chooses the right road, a fool takes the wrong one" Ecclesiastes 10:2 (NLT). We can reach out, believe God, and allow Him to help us through the situation, or we can turn our back on God, becoming hard and bitter.

Personal Note:

We can go through many difficult things not necessarily of our own making. There are times when someone else's decisions change the course of our own lives dramatically and forcefully, such as what happened on September 11, 2001. That changed the course of the whole world and it will never be the same again.

I have gone through some fierce personal battles, as I know most of us have. Nevertheless, my heavenly Father has always reached down, gathered me up in His strong arms, and held me close to His heart to cherish and strengthen me through the trial. When it was over, I have become stronger both physically and spiritually. His justice is always tempered with mercy.

Sometimes I have to simply trust Him. No matter how much I hate going through the trial that God has allowed or how much I do not understand, I can rest in the assurance that He is always just. Even though it is extremely painful, I am so much closer to my heavenly Father because of what I have endured. No matter what the circumstance, God is just and He always will take care of me through the hard challenges of life. David wrote, "The Lord is just! He is my rock! There is no evil in Him" Psalm 92:15 (NLT).

Prayer:

Oh Father, how hard it is at times to simply trust You even though I know You are always just. Help me as I go through my trials to put my trust in You because You alone can sustain me. In Jesus' name, Amen.

Your Reflections:

Day 26

God is . . . Guardian of My Heart

Bible Reading: Psalm 16:5-9

No matter what the situation, God is always there to guard my heart and soul, and keep me safe from the stresses of life. That does not mean that I am untouchable. I go through some tough times, but though I am surrounded by the trials of life, God is there protecting and guarding my heart so that He can help me through the rough spots.

I love the way Psalm 16:5 is worded in the *New Living Translation*, "Lord You alone are my inheritance, my cup of blessing. You guard all that is mine." The enemy may strike, but I can have confidence in knowing that God Himself is guarding everything that is mine. He is my "cup of blessing" among the stresses of life!

Peter talks about the loving guardianship of Christ in I Peter 2:25 "Once you were like sheep who wandered away. But now you have turned to your Shepherd, the Guardian of your souls." (NLT). What a great reminder that Christ is always with us watching over our hearts against whatever storm may arise.

Personal Note:

From my journal on March 11, 2000: "It is so easy to lose my focus when I am hurting or in need. I cry out to my God; but sometimes it is hard to trust that He hears me. I am so absorbed in the problem that I forget He is always there. I become more focused on my own needs and am unable to relax and just let Him carry my burden."

That is exactly what He wants to do. He wants to guard my heart and carry my load. Relinquishing my control to Him is always the right answer! So many things resolve themselves when I leave them in His care.

I was recently in a very stressful situation. I had a conversation with someone, which resulted in a terrible misunderstanding, I felt awful! I prayed and trusted the Guardian of my heart.

Within minutes, I had two wonderful phone calls that helped change my whole attitude—one from my son and one from a very good friend whom I had not talked to in a while. Coincidence? I don't think so! I believe that my Shepherd was watching over me and helping me get my focus back on Him.

I will always have struggles in my life. That is normal however; it is the way in which I handle the struggles that will bring about my personal growth. Do I turn it over into His capable hands, or do I try to carry it myself? The choice is always mine!

Prayer:

Father, I thank You that you guard my heart and help me through every situation. Help me to trust You and be more in tune with Your heart as I grow closer to You each step of the way. In Jesus' name, Amen.

Your Reflections:

Day 27

God is . . . Divine Power

Bible Reading: II Peter 1:1-6

Divine Power. This attribute refers only to God. The word divine is such a holy word that it is not used often in scripture. When it is used, it helps describe the sacredness and power of God. Peter describes this, "By His divine power, God has given us everything we need for living a godly life. We have received all of this by coming to know Him, the One who called us to Himself by means of His marvelous glory and excellence" II Peter 1:3 (NLT).

We get to share in God's divine nature because of Christ! "And because of His glory and excellence He has given us great and precious promises. These are the promises that enable us to share His divine nature and escape the world's corruption caused by human desires" II Peter 1:4 (NLT).

Think of it! We can escape all of the corruption that surrounds us. However, in order to do that, we must be totally committed and submitted to God's purpose and plan for our lives. The more of *us* we turn over to His care, the more we are protected from all of the corruption that we must face every day. This does not mean that we are placed in a bubble in our own little world and we never venture out or around anyone that is not in our own little safe circle—No! We are to be lights in a dark world.

We are to be "in" the world but not "of" the world. Paul makes a strong statement in his letter to the Corinthians. "The weapons we fight with are not the weapons of the world; on the contrary, they have divine power to demolish strongholds" II Corinthians 10:4 (NIV). At the end of verse six Paul continues: "We can do this when our obedience is complete." In other words, as we grow in the Lord and become closer to Him, He will enable us with divine power to fight the enemy of this world! That is a very strong statement. We can see the power of darkness all around us, but we do not have to be a part of it. What a blessing!

Personal Note:

It is amazing how Satan and my own nature keep trying to make me unworthy to just step out in God's divine power and keep writing this devotional. The many hours that I spend working on this keeps my mind focused on the Lord and His plan for me. I don't think anyone realizes more than I, how very incapable I am of doing this on my own. I just keep writing and know it is God-directed, because this is impossible to do by my own strength. I wouldn't even attempt or think of doing something like this. What a God I serve! How powerful! How divine!

Prayer:

Thank You, Father, for Your holiness and power. You take me places that I never could dream of when I am willing to let You turn loose Your sublime nature and omnipotence within me. Help me to walk worthy of this calling. In Jesus' name, Amen.

Your Reflections:

Day 28

God is . . . My Tear-Gatherer

Bible Reading: Psalm 56:8-13

Can we even imagine how much God cares for us? He understands all about our hurts and sorrows.

I'm not sure that many of us like to be around someone who is crying. It is very distressing. We may try to comfort them, but to understand their situation is at times challenging and uncomfortable.

What do we say to a friend or relative who has just lost someone dear to them? I have suffered many losses of loved ones in my life and been around very close friends who have gone through some horrible losses. It is always a heart-wrenching time. Whether you are going through something or supporting someone else through distress, there is only so much anyone else can do. The person experiencing the loss is the only one who knows exactly what they are going through and feeling.

Nevertheless, God not only knows about every heartache and heartbreak, He cares in a way that no human can. He created us. "Oh, Lord, You have searched me and known me. You know my sitting down and my rising up. You understand my thought afar off. You comprehend my path and my lying down, and are acquainted with all my ways. For there is not a word on my tongue, but behold, O Lord, You know it altogether" Psalm 139:1-4 (NKJ).

A God who knows us that well knows about our tears and sadness. "You keep track of all my sorrows. You have collected all my tears in Your bottle. You have recorded each one in Your book" Psalm 56:8 (NLT). What an image that verse creates. We cannot hurt so deeply that God does not understand. He collects our tears and counts them one by one.

Personal Note:

Yes, I have known personal loss. I lost a cousin when he was 5 years old to a hit-and-run drunk driver. I had two sisters killed in a head-on collision when they were in their thirties. My father passed away from cancer at age fifty-six. I went through the loss of all of my aunts and uncles and most of my cousins. All of these bereavements happened by the time I was sixty years old. My husband and I have lost both our parents and thought we were going to lose our daughter at age sixteen.

It is so comforting for me to know that my Father has a big bottle for my tears. He counts every one of them. I'm sure that they number in the thousands by now. Nevertheless, every time He has brought me through the deep waters and wiped away my tears. I have great comfort in knowing that no matter what I face, He will be there to collect my tears one by one in that bottle and strengthen me as I go through it. When I reach the other side there is always victory in Him!

Prayer:

Oh Father, I come to You knowing that someone is out there today hurting very badly. Help them through this dreadful time to know that You are with them. I'm so grateful to You that You keep track of my sorrows and collect my tears. Thank you for caring so much about me. In Jesus' name, Amen.

Your Reflections:

Day 29

God is . . . Trustworthy

Bible Reading: Luke 16:10-13

Trustworthiness! This is a great challenge for our society today. What is being "trustworthy?" Webster defines it as being dependable, or reliable. It is keeping our word. When we say we are going to do something, if we are trustworthy, we will do it! In our bustling life style, it is easy to tell people that we will call them, or pray for them. Do we follow through? If we tell someone that we will do something, God expects us to do it, whether or not other things come up or get in the way.

How empty our words can be! We may have the best of intentions but if we do not follow through, we compromise someone's trust in us. We may make excuses, but truthfully, we devalue the importance of our commitment to that person. We may have greatly inconvenienced those who have been waiting for us to fulfill our word. This can be very hurtful and can harm our relationship. If we communicate to others that they are important to us, and do not keep our promises it is hard for them to have confidence in us. It feels to them like we may not care as much as we say.

Our Bible reading today refers to money, but I think it applies to our everyday life as well. In verse ten it reads, "Whoever can be trusted with very little can also be trusted with much, and whoever is dishonest with very little will also be dishonest with much" (NIV). God is trustworthy and He expects us to learn to be as well.

Wow! Trying to live this one out can really hurt! Trustworthiness is very important as we walk with our Lord. He is always faithful to His word. The Bible is full of examples of God keeping His word. "Your word, O Lord, is eternal; it stands firm in the heavens" Psalm 119:89

(NIV). God is always and forever reliable. It is so good to remember that even though we fail, God never does!

Personal Note:

This was a very hard message to write. In fact, I tried to change it to another topic. Talk about God directing my path! I have been so guilty at times of this. It is definitely an area that still needs work. However, my heavenly Father is merciful and He is helping me understand where I need to change. I have been working diligently on staying true to my word.

We are all so busy and we just flippantly say, "I'll call you later," or "I will see you tomorrow," and then we either forget or have other priorities. I think the hardest lesson to admit is, if I tell somebody something and don't do it, I compromise my integrity and trustworthiness with that person. I need to guard my lips so that I do not make commitments that I cannot keep.

Prayer:

O Father, please forgive me for being flippant with my words. Help me learn to be more trustworthy, as You are trustworthy. Help me to be committed to follow through with what I say. In Jesus' Name, Amen.

Your Reflections:

Day 30

God is . . . Our Planner

Bible Reading: Genesis 45:3-8

One of the great examples of God fulfilling His plan is the story of Joseph. When he was still a boy he used to dream, and in some of his dreams God would give him a clear picture of what would happen in the future. At one point, he not only told his dream to his brothers and father, but there may have been a little taunting in his tone.

His brothers already were very jealous of him because he was their father's favorite. (Joseph's dreams that someday he would rule over all of them, including his father, made the brothers hate him.) You may know the story. Jacob made Joseph a coat of many colors setting him apart as even more special. I cannot help but wonder if he held that over his brothers every chance he got. Anyway, the story goes on to tell how the brothers sold Joseph to a caravan going to Egypt. Joseph became a slave, but God's protection allowed him to be head of the household of an important dignitary, Potiphar.

After the wife of Potiphar tried to seduce Joseph and he refused, she lied to her husband and blamed Joseph for trying to rape her. Joseph was thrown into prison where he remained for three years. Then Pharaoh had a dream that none of his experts could tell him; his butler who had been in prison with Joseph, remembered the skills he had shown in prison. Joseph interpreted Pharaoh's dream. As a result, Pharaoh appointed Joseph to the position of the second most powerful man in all of Egypt.

There was a horrible famine in the land that even affected Jacob and all his family who were living in the land of Canaan. The brothers ended up going to Egypt and bowing down to Joseph whom they did not recognize, thus fulfilling God's plan all along!

It took many years for God to build Joseph's character to be adept at fulfilling what God had created him to be. I imagine that he was quite spoiled as a child. In order to use him in such an incredible way, God had to allow Joseph to "grow up" and learn some lessons! We read in Genesis 45:7 (NLT). "God has sent me ahead of you to keep you and your families alive and to preserve many survivors." Joseph even learned true forgiveness. There was no resentment toward his brothers, just pure love.

Personal Note:

As I look at my own life, I can see systematically how God brought me to this special time where He can use me in this unique way—beyond my wildest dreams. God knew before I was born that I would be writing this, even though I didn't have a "clue." As I look back, I can see the preparation that was involved.

Six years ago, I started on this new journey to get to know the Father; but even before that, I had a period of time when I wrote poetry. I still do occasionally and have written a couple of short allegorical stories. However, I never really thought about doing serious writing. In fact, I always said that my poetry is God's poetry, because I never felt that I had a knack for writing.

Nonetheless, I come from a very artistic family. My grandfather was a traveling preacher who wrote music and had a song published, grandmother was an artist and many of us have her art hanging in our homes. My aunts and uncle wrote poetry and one aunt was an artist. Mother wrote a very artistic work that she called "A Quick Trip through the Bible." It was all visually illustrated. My sister does scripts for plays.

Chris our son is an artist and writer; he helped my mother with some of her illustrations for her project. Jill, our daughter is not only a writer, but also a conference speaker who travels all over the world. She also has several Bible studies in print.

Did God have a plan for me? Absolutely! I am still in awe of what He is doing in my life! Moreover, He has a plan designed for you as well! Jeremiah wrote, "For I know the plans I have for you. They are plans for good and not for disaster, to give you a future and a hope" Jeremiah 29:11 (NLT). Like Joseph, God had much preparation within me to bring me to this place and I still don't know where He is going with this writing, but it is not mine to know. I must only obey and keep writing!

Prayer:

Oh my Father, You truly are an awesome God. You know everything about me and the plans that You have for me. I pray that You will continue to use me in whatever purpose You have for my life. In Jesus' name, Amen.

Your Reflections:

Day 31

God is . . . My Source

Bible Reading: Psalm 42:1-5

I love this quality of my heavenly Father, my source! He is the starting point, the new beginnings of our faith. Whether we have come into a recent relationship with Him, or if we have failed Him in our walk, we need only reach out to Him and He will be there to give us a fresh start. He is our source every day and in everything that we do.

David was called "a man after God's own heart." Yet in many of his psalms, we read of his despair, helplessness and hopelessness. He always remembered his source, however, and came with a repentant heart and deep sorrow in the realization that he had failed His God. David wrote, "I waited patiently for the Lord; He turned to me and heard my cry. He lifted me out of the slimy pit, out of the mud and mire; He set my feet on a rock and gave me a firm place to stand" Psalm 40:1-2 (NIV). Yes, David knew his source!

When I think of God as my source, I like the definition that He is my "point of supply." How fully He fits this concept. He is the source of supply. He gives abundantly for anyone who, by faith, asks in His name and for His purpose. I chose today's passage of scripture because it so beautifully portrays the source of rich supply that our Father provides and how I respond to Him. "As the deer pants for streams of water, so my soul pants for you, O God" Psalm 42:1 (NIV).

I have been to the beginning of a stream, just walking in nature with no water in sight; and then all of a sudden, out of nowhere bubbles a ripple of water that immediately feeds itself and becomes a stream. It is so beautiful! The psalmist wrote, "You make springs pour water into the ravines, so streams gush down from the mountains" Psalm 104:10 (NLT). What a good example of what happens to us sometimes.

We can become dry and downhearted, but when we let God take over, streams of living water flow freely through us. Next thing we know, we are bubbling over with His mercy and joy!

Personal Note:

Sometimes, like David, I feel parched and dry. Nevertheless, it is always refreshing and renewing when I come to my Father with a penitent heart and ask Him to forgive my thoughts or actions. He fills me from His source, gives me a new starting point. He never fails to supply me with His abundant love and grace. Then He restores my soul and brings me back to the still waters of His mercy and I have a new beginning with Him at the center where He belongs. There is nothing in the world that can bring that kind of peace, contentment and joy!

Prayer:

Father, I know that sometimes I get ahead of You and Your plan for me. I thank You because You are an ever-living source of forgiveness and blessing and I'm grateful that You fill me and restore my soul. Help me to learn to seek You first in every situation. In Jesus' name, Amen.

Your Reflections:

Day 32

God is . . . All Sufficient

Bible Reading: 2 Corinthians 12:7-12

We get so self-absorbed sometimes that we do not rely on our all-sufficient God. My mother used to call it "the big I." We all have a tendency to do this at times. Sometimes our heavenly Father allows difficult things to come into our lives so that we will come to Him with our needs. We must realize that He is the only one who is sufficient to take care of whatever trial we are facing.

The Apostle Paul experienced this. He had an incredible vision that caused him to want to tell everyone about it. God showed him that doing so, would create a boastful attitude so Paul refrained from telling people about it. What was this amazing vision? He was caught up into the third heaven where he saw such astounding things that they could not be expressed in words. He wrote in verse five, "That experience is worth boasting about, but I'm not going to do it. I will boast only about my weakness" (NLT).

Would we be tempted to boast about such a fabulous experience? I think many of us would try to tell someone! We are so self-centered that we love to tell great things about ourselves. Some of us even like to boast about wonderful things that the Lord has done for us. When people compliment us on the experience, we tend to thank them, which then becomes boasting in ourselves, and not giving God all the glory. In verse nine we read, "But He said to me, My grace is sufficient for you, for My power is made perfect in weakness" (NIV).

Yes, God can use us most effectively when we are weak. That is because when we admit that we are helpless and cry out for His help, we know that only God can take care of the situation. "But God chose the foolish things of the world to shame the wise; God chose the weak things of the world to shame the strong" I Corinthians 1:27 (NIV). He now has the empty vessel that He needs to fulfill His purpose in us. He alone is sufficient for the need.

Personal Note:

From my journal on April 15, 2000: "In times of need, what is the first thing I do? I usually pray and ask for God's help at some point, but not always until I have tried to fix it myself. I forget sometimes to praise Him and say, 'Lord, no matter how difficult things get, "Your grace is sufficient for me. You are all I need.' He is always there waiting patiently with His arms wide open. All I need to do is step into the comfort of those arms and stay close to Him. When I do, the burden is light."'

I have grown in this area, but I am still learning to run to those open arms sooner and let Him encompass me with His grace and sufficiency, and to allow Him to take care of the problem or the hurt, letting Him heal my wounded heart and make me whole again. Wholeness is His ultimate goal for me. He is all that I need. I just have to learn to go to Him immediately, so that I do not needlessly suffer anxiety or pain because "His yoke is easy and His burden is light!" Matthew 11:30 (NIV).

Prayer:

Father, it is so easy to depend on myself instead of Your sufficiency. When I do, things often turn out to be a real mess. Lord, teach me to lean on Your adequacy even though the lesson may be hard to learn. In Jesus' name, Amen.

Your Reflections:

Day 33

God is . . . Fullness

Bible Reading: Colossians 2:6-10

If we want to know God in His fullness, we need only look at His Son, Jesus, who saved us by His grace. In our passage today we read, "For in Christ lives all the fullness of God in a human body" Colossians 2:9 (NLT). That puts everything in perspective. Fullness means completeness. It is what we need to stop the yearning and the unrest we feel deep within our being.

Sometimes we do not experience this kind of relationship with God because we really do not want to be filled up with Him. We may be too afraid of letting go of something that we are controlling. We all struggle with this in certain areas, I am sure, because none of us is perfect.

We use the expression "she is really full of herself" and what we mean is that the person is self-centered or self-fulfilled. Their center or grounding is inward.

That was Lucifer's problem before he fell from grace. He was centered on himself and so wanted to be as great or greater than God was. He had everything in heaven. He was called the "son of the morning." He knew that He was a very important and beautiful creation and he became full of himself, instead of God. That was his literal downfall. We read in Isaiah 14:12-13 (NKJ), "'How you are fallen from heaven, O Lucifer, son of the morning! How you are cut down to the ground, you who weakened the nations!' For you have said in your heart: 'I will ascend into heaven, I will exalt my throne above the stars of God; I will also sit on the mount of the congregation. On the farthest sides of the north; I will ascend above the heights of the clouds, I will be like the Most High.'"

God hates self-centeredness because it minimizes His ability to give us the fullness of His glory. We who are made in His likeness, desire His fullness. That is how we were made. It is the core purpose of our existence. That is why when we try to fill our lives with self-gratification, we never feel satisfied. Paul wrote, "If anyone thinks he is something when he is nothing, he deceives himself" Galatians 6:3 (NIV). Only God can fill our lives and make us complete.

Personal Note:

From my journal on April 16, 2000: "Knowing God in His fullness is in our power if we put God first and do not add something else to Him. He is the center of our existence. As I learn to do this, my thinking changes and the "Big I" disappears."

There are many things that can take first place (be an idol) in my life. I think of idols as being made of wood, stone or an icon that is worshipped. I do not do that so therefore I don't think I have any idols in my life. That is not how God sees it. How do I know an idol in my life? If deep down inside, at the center of my existence, my foundation is on anything other than God, that is an idol.

He does not like being on the "back burner" of my heart. When God is the center or the stability on which everything else flows, then other things are more fulfilling than I ever imagined. His blessings are so prevalent in my life that it overflows with His fullness and every desire I ever had is multiplied.

Prayer:

Oh Father, this is a tough lesson. You made me to love, worship and have real communication with You. Nothing other than You can ever fulfill me. Please forgive me when I do not allow You first place in my life. Help me to release anything that is above You, and to seek Your fullness in my life. In Jesus' name, Amen.

Your Reflections:

Day 34

God is . . . One In Unity

Bible Reading: Ephesians 4:2-6

Unity is something that pleases God. He created us to be individuals, but be united in our spirits. He never meant for us, especially Christians, to be at odds with each other. At times, though, we are the ones who are the most critical of our brothers and sisters.

Christ died so that we could all come to Him and live with Him forever. Too often, we forget the ultimate goal and let our differences take over. In Ephesians we read, "With all lowliness and gentleness, with longsuffering, bearing with one another in love, endeavoring to keep the unity of the Spirit in the bond of peace" Ephesians 4:2-3 (NKJ).

We are each so unique. Sometimes our differences put a wedge in the spirit of unity that we were created to have and too often, our brothers and sisters in the Lord are our worst critics. Sometimes personalities clash and people do not get along too well. Nevertheless, God wants us to preserve the spirit of unity above protecting our own personal feelings.

It is so sad to see church members split off and start a new church simply because of a difference of opinion. We are to love each other and lay aside our differences for the greater good, which is our love for our Lord and the work that He wants us to do.

The Trinity is very different in nature and yet perfect in unity. God wants us to follow what He has modeled for us, so that we may reap the greatest of blessing and reward.

We are all sinners, and letting our differences override our unity is not what God wants for us. Jesus talked about this in the Sermon on the Mount. "And why do you look at the speck in your brother's eye, but do not consider the plank in your own eye?" Matthew 7:3 (NKJ). It is so easy to find fault with each other, yet it is a lot harder to find oneness. But what a great goal!

Personal Note:

One of the areas that I have tried to guard against is a critical spirit. I think I have grown over the years because as I have seen what turmoil can be created by dissension, I don't want any part of it. However, I think it is easy for us to become critical of someone and it can create so much pain. Even if we thoughtlessly make a bad comment about one of our sisters or brothers in the faith, it can be very hurtful. Many people have left a church and "never set foot in one again," just because of something that was said. God wants me to guard my tongue and love and support others in the unity of the Spirit.

Prayer:

Oh Father, please search my own heart as you are teaching me all of these areas that are so hard to talk about. May You guard my tongue and help me to love others as You love. In Jesus' name, Amen.

Your Reflections:

Day 35

God is . . . Bounteous

Bible Reading: Psalm 36:5-9

I live in Oregon where in early April nature is so vivid. It seems like each day when I awaken there is just a little more color. The daffodils and jonquils bloom, the trees blossom, and the very young and tender leaves spring forth with new life on bushes and trees. After a winter of rest, God's creation comes alive. I love all the seasons as they come and go; but spring, the sign of new growth—how magnificent it is!

Webster describes bounteous as "abundant, giving generously, plentiful." I personally don't think any of these words are strong enough to apply to what God is toward us and all that we have available through Him. I used bounteous because to me it sounds bigger and greater than bountiful. No matter what word I use, God is everything I could ever imagine and way beyond anything my mind can conjure up. My human mind cannot fathom Him.

Our Father is indescribably and limitlessly bountiful. Most of the time we don't even scratch the surface of all He wants to bestow on us. He is bountiful in love, in grace, in mercy, in blessing, in provision, and so much more However, the best example of His bounteous love was when He gave His only Son to die for us and forgive us for our sins.

When we describe God as bounteous, we normally think of provision but His wonderful bounty is seen in nature as well. Moses wrote, "Listen, O heavens and I will speak; hear, O earth, the words of my mouth. Let my teaching fall like rain, and my words descend like dew, like showers on new grass, like abundant rain on tender plants" Deuteronomy 32:1-2 (NIV).

It is interesting that David used nature to help describe some of God's bounty. "Your love, O Lord, reaches to the heavens, Your faithfulness to the skies, Your righteousness is like the mighty mountains, Your justice like the great deep" Psalm 36:5-6 (NIV). Yes, His creation is bounteous in beauty, but it is only a glimpse of what is available to us here on earth as well as what is waiting for us when we get to heaven!

Personal Note:

God has blessed me with so much beauty all around me in a bountiful display. I forget sometimes in the busyness of my life to enjoy the beauty God has provided for me. My daughter, Jill lives in the desert; and even there, nature comes alive and His bounty is seen in the spring as the cactus break forth in beautiful blooms and the desert is alive with abundant color.

I am so blessed to see the breaking forth of springtime in Oregon, I love to see the spectacular liveliness of the sky. There is blue sky, gray sky, billowing white fluffy clouds, dark threatening cloud, which produce wonderful rain showers and yes, rainbows! It is common to see a triple rainbow, each one becoming less vivid in color than the first. I have not even covered the depth of colors in the sky itself. The sunrises and sunsets, the depth of blue that is so vivid at times it almost seems purple. What a blessing He provides as He paints such a beautiful picture of His bountifulness in our sky!

God has certainly provided us with His bounteous love of nature and color and so much variety to look at. Even when I am at my busiest, I cannot help observing and praising Him for the beauty all around me. He is truly bountiful in blessing us in so many ways.

Prayer:

Father, I lift up my spirit to You and praise You for Your bounteous love that sent Your Son to earth to die for me. I also want to praise You for the beauty that You surround me with every day. You are truly awesome in all Your ways. Thank you with all my heart. In my Savior's name, Amen.

Your Reflections:

Day 36

God is . . . The Glorious Presence

Bible Reading: Exodus 33:17-23

God's glory is so magnificent that we can never look upon His face. Moses came the nearest to seeing God's glory. When he was leading the children of Israel through the wilderness, the people were so rebellious that Moses often had to plead with God so that He would not destroy them. The worst time was after God had called Moses to go up onto Mt. Sinai. There the finger of God wrote out the Ten Commandments on tablets of stone for the people to follow. Can you even imagine having God personally write something out for you in His own handwriting?

The people became impatient because Moses was gone too long. So they asked Aaron to make a golden calf out of all the gold they collected from jewelry and objects from the people. I don't know why Aaron agreed but he was not a leader, he was a priest, and the people must have overwhelmed him. However, he did as the people asked. When Moses heard all of the wild celebrating that was going on, and then saw what they were doing, he was so angry that he threw the tablets down on the ground, smashing them.

If Moses was this angry, we cannot even imagine how angry God was! Moses interceded for Israel to keep God from destroying them. God must punish sin, so He sent a great plague upon the people and many died.

It was after this event that Moses pleaded with God to show him His glorious presence. In verse seventeen of the New Living Translation we read, "The Lord replied to Moses, I will indeed do what you have asked, for I look favorably on you, and I know you by name. However, God ends in verses 22-23 by saying, "As My glorious presence passes by, I will hide you in the crevice of the rock and cover you with My hand, until I have passed by. Then I will remove My hand and let you see Me from behind. But My face will not be seen." Even seeing that much of God, Moses' countenance was so bright that he had to wear a covering over his face because the people could not look on him because of his brightness. What a glorious presence we have to look forward to, when our mortal bodies will be changed to immortal and we can really see God face to face.

Personal Note:

I can only imagine what that must have been like for Moses. But God gives us glimpses of His magnificent glory when we come to Him in prayer and worship. When we have an intimate encounter with the glorious presence of our Father, we can do nothing else but worship Him. His presence is so strong that without covering us with His hand, we could not tolerate the power of His glory.

As I grow in Him, I indeed find favor with Him, and I long to stay a little longer in His presence. Each step I take toward Him brings me closer to His glory. I want to keep growing, so that I might experience Him deeper and deeper. I am so thankful that He loves me so much that He desires this experience for me even more than I do.

Prayer:

Father, I feel so favored by You right now that I cannot help but worship Your mightiness. What an awesome privilege You give me to come directly into Your presence and worship because of Christ's sacrifice on the cross. I thank You in His name, Amen.

Your Reflections:

Day 37

God is . . . Holy

Bible Reading: Hebrews 12:18-24

People around us take God, and the things of God, very lightly every day. There is a lack of reverence and holiness; and most of us have no idea about the intricate workings of God and His kingdom. There is nothing or no one that exists who is holy, except God. If we had only one word to describe Him, it would be holy. He wants us to live holy lives, as He is holy.

As sinful man there is only one way to do that, and that is through the shed blood of Jesus Christ who paid for our sins and provided for our righteousness on the cross. He paid every physical and spiritual debt that we could ever have in our lives.

Hebrews gives such a wonderful description of the reverence and holiness with which we come before our God. "You have come to Mount Zion, to the city of the living God, the heavenly Jerusalem, and to countless thousands of angels in a joyful gathering. You have come to the assembly of God's firstborn children, whose names are written in heaven. You have come to God Himself, who is the judge over all things. You have come to the spirits of the righteous ones in heaven who have now been made perfect. You have come to Jesus, the One who mediates the new covenant between God and people, and to the sprinkled blood, which speaks of forgiveness instead of crying out for vengeance like the blood of Abel" Hebrews 12:22-24 (NLT). What a gorgeous picture of what is going on in heaven.

When we come before Him in reverence and purity, worshiping Him, just think of all of the beings who are bowing before His throne. They are all rejoicing, worshiping, and praising as a joyful gathering. I know that all of my family and my husband's family, who have gone on before us, are part of that joyful celebration. "Since we are receiving a Kingdom that is unshakeable, let us be thankful and please God by worshiping Him with holy fear and awe" Hebrews 12:28 (NLT). What a day of rejoicing that will be when I stand with all those who went before me and worship my holy and awesome Father!

Personal Note:

I am sure that I haven't any idea what heaven is like. I don't think any human can really know what awaits us. The daily work and worship that goes on, the glory, and the reverence that the angels display and the joy that all the ones who have gone on before us have for our Creator, I admit that I have not even thought about heaven in that depth before.

I wonder how many of us truly have thought about heaven in this way. I don't remember hearing a sermon preached on this, at least not in the way it is pictured in the New Living Translation of the Bible. Maybe it is because of where I am now in relationship with Him, that this strikes me as such a beautiful and wondrous thing. Nonetheless, I am so thankful that I serve a holy Father who has a working organized routine that goes on daily in heaven and yet still has time to love me with an everlasting love. "Love so amazing, so divine—demands my soul, my life, my all."

Prayer:

Oh Father, As I begin to understand a little of what is awaiting me in Your heavenly city of Zion, how it humbles me as I come before You, who are so holy and divine. I can hardly wait to be among the righteous ones who are made perfect through Christ. You are truly worthy to be praised! I worship You and adore You. In the precious name of Jesus, Amen.

Your Reflections:

Day 38

God is . . . A Message-Transmitter

Bible Reading: Isaiah 52:7-10

God has always had messengers. The angels do His bidding day and night. "For He will command His angels concerning you, to guard you in all your ways" Psalm 91:11 (NIV). What comfort that brings to us to know that God commands angels to watch over us personally. That is just a small part of what His messengers do.

The first angel He ever sent to earth was to the garden of Eden. That was after Adam and Eve sinned and God banished them from the garden. He placed Cherubim with a flaming sword to guard the tree of life, so that Adam and Eve could no longer have access to it and live forever.

We have many accounts in the Bible, especially in the Old Testament, of angels visiting a particular individual and relaying a message to them from God Almighty! I think Abraham may have been the first. However, there is a long line of messengers that God sent as a way to communicate a specific message.

In the New Testament, the best-known account, is when an angel visited Mary the mother of Jesus. However, Jesus Himself is the ultimate messenger. The greatest message ever told is Jesus Himself. And what a message and messenger He is! Because of His willingness to be the ultimate sacrifice on the cross to pay for our sins, God the Father exalts Him, as He will no other. Christ is the only one who sits at the right hand of the Father. He is the only one who is King of kings and Lord of lords.

I chose today's reading because it is a great description of our heavenly Lord. "How beautiful on the mountain are the feet of the messenger who brings good news, good news of peace and salvation, the news that the God of Israel reigns" Isaiah 52:7 (NLT).

His word to us today comes through the holy Word of God, the Bible. He also wants to use us as His messengers to a lost world. The Great Commission speaks to us even today. "Therefore go and make disciples of all nations, baptizing them in the name of the Father and of the Son and of the Holy Spirit, and teaching them to obey everything I have commanded you. And surely I am with you always, to the very end of the age" Matthew 28:19,20 (NIV).

Personal Note:

From my journal on April 27, 2000: "As I am growing (ever so slowly) in His way, one of my biggest challenges is speaking openly and publicly about my faith. God is dealing with me on this point. He has blessed me abundantly with so many things that my heart wants to proclaim Him and praise Him. But I cannot do this within my own strength. I need a touch from the Master and boldness from the Holy Spirit; then I can carry His message effectively."

I am much more comfortable now with talking about the One who has so drastically changed my life. And who knows, maybe this book is yet another way to proclaim His name!

Prayer:

Thank You, Father, for sending the Ultimate Messenger, that I might have access to Your throne through Jesus Christ my Lord. I thank You that You are using me even in small ways. I pray that in whatever You have for me, I will be obedient to Your call. In my Savior's name, Amen.

Your Reflections:

Day 39

God is . . . Praise Loving

Bible Reading: Psalm 100:1-5

God loves praise! Why should He not? He has blessed us so abundantly that praise should be on our lips all the time. The Psalms are full of acclamation to God.

I chose today's passage for a very personal reason. This was the psalm that my grandfather put to music and it was later published. I referred to grandpa's song on another day, but today I wanted to focus on the psalm about which He wrote. Psalm 100 because it is filled with thanksgiving, joy and praise to our heavenly Father.

It reads, "Shout for joy to the Lord, all the earth. Worship the Lord with gladness; come before Him with joyful song. Know that the Lord is God. It is He who made us and we are His; we are His people, the sheep of His pasture. Enter His gates with thanksgiving and His courts with praise; give thanks to Him and praise His name. For the Lord is good and His love endures forever; His faithfulness continues through all generations" Psalm 100:1-5 (NIV). One of the things that strike me in this psalm is that we enter the gates of His heavenly city with thanksgiving, but we do not enter the courts without praise. Imagine! We get to be much closer to our Father when we give Him praise!

Personal Note:

Praise is something that God adores. He loves me to elevate and appreciate Him. He blesses those who extol Him. This is one of the ways that I have grown in my prayer life. It is so amazing to me, because I have always been afraid to pray aloud in public. I would hear the prayer all around me that was worded so beautifully and from the heart, and I always felt inadequate because my prayer was always so simple.

It was not until I heard a speaker one time talk about how important praise is to God that I started to grow in this area. He said, "It is a good thing, if we are not used to really praising Him, to start out by just appreciating Him for a few seconds. Then increase the time as we become more comfortable." As I started to do this, I began to feel very comfortable talking to my Father aloud. My problem was not what other people were saying in their prayer; it was my self-centered nature, getting in the way of real fellowship with God. Now I praise Him all the time. It is just a natural and special part of my day. I praise Him many times throughout the day.

Prayer:

My heavenly Father, how I glorify You today for the pure joy of just praising You. You have done so much for me but, most importantly, I appreciate You for sending Your Son Jesus Christ into my life, so that I might have a way to come before You in praise. Thank you, in His blessed name, Amen.

Your Reflections:

Day 40

God is . . . Worthy of Worship

Bible Reading: Psalm 29:1-5

Worship and praise go hand in hand. Just as God loves praise, He loves worship. David wrote, "Honor the Lord for the glory of His name. Worship the Lord in the splendor of His holiness" Psalm 29:2 (NLT). Whenever we worship (come before Him with reverence and awe because of who He is), and praise (pay Him respect and gratitude for what He has done), God brings us to the inner circle of His love.

Have you ever been in the "inner circle" of a church, organization or business? That is where all of the confidence and vision come from, and where plans are born and carried out. Sometimes when we are in the inner circle, especially in a church body, we tend to forget the outer circle of people. This is not a good thing. Nevertheless, when we are in God's inner circle with the praise and worshippers there is only peace and joy.

When we leave the inner circle and enter the outer circle of every day life, we take the blessing with us and include all those around us. There is no exclusiveness with God. He wants all those who know Him to come and worship Him. Worship is the place where we honor our Father. Worship is the place of joy and adoration. Adulation, many times, includes singing. When we truly come to God in prayer, with praise and worship, He honors us in a very special way.

David knew firsthand how to worship his King. When he was facing enemies or difficult trials, the first thing he did was turn to God. He wrote, "You have turned my mourning into joyful dancing. You have taken away my clothes of mourning and clothed me with joy, that I might sing praises to You and not be silent, O Lord my God, I will give You thanks forever" Psalm 30:11,12 (NLT). What a blessing there is in worship!

Personal Note:

It is so exciting that we exist to worship God. That is why He created us. He did not create us so that we would be famous painters, or fabulous singers known worldwide, or Chairman in a large Company. No! He created us to worship Him in the beauty of holiness, to have an intimate relationship with Him.

It is awesome as I grow spiritually, to know without a shadow of a doubt that I am in the presence of God Almighty and can worship Him along with the angels and all the other believers who are also worshipping Him. It doesn't matter to God whether I am a famous well-known Christian figure, like Billy Graham, or just a 72-year-old woman, who loves her Lord and wants fellowship with Him. I can delight in Him as reverently as anyone, no matter the fame, and be equally honored by Him. We hold people in high esteem. God holds worship in high esteem! What a privilege it is to know that each one of us is equal in His love.

Prayer:

Oh, Father, what a privilege to carry everything to You in prayer. I honor You and worship You. You are truly exalted above all. I thank You for Your Son who died that I might have the joy of worshipping You. You are truly worthy of worship! In His name, Amen.

Your Reflections:

Day 41

God is . . . The Shining Treasure

Bible Reading: 2 Corinthians 4:5-8

As Christians, we are fragile and very vulnerable to Satan's charms. However, when God saved us He sent the Holy Spirit to live in us and He became our strength. He fills us up so that we can then be poured out in the newness of His light. I love what Paul wrote, "We now have this light shining in our hearts, but we ourselves are like fragile clay jars containing this great treasure" 2 Corinthians 4:7 (NLT).

I picture in my mind a clay pot that may have been around the hot blistering sun too long. It has many cracks and is hardened by the environment. There is One who not only can mend the pot, but also fill it up to its fullest capacity. Even then, it will continually run over with this wonderful treasure of light.

When Christ ascended to heaven He told the disciples, "And now I will send the Holy Spirit, just as my Father promised. But stay here in the city until the Holy Spirit comes and fills you with power from heaven" Luke 24:49 (NLT). Christ knew that without the power of the Holy Spirit we would not be able to withstand the temptations and trials of our lives. We would give in to our own selfish desires. That is one of Satan's biggest weapons—our own selfish nature.

We are all *cracked jars*; however, the beauty of God's Holy Spirit cannot only fill us up, His beauty will shine through the cracks! We don't have to be perfect before God's power and light can shine through in our lives. While we are allowing His cleansing to heal the cracks, His light glows through them and fills us up to capacity. We read in I John 1:7, "But if we are living in the light, as God is in the light, then we have fellowship with each other, and the blood of Jesus, His Son, cleanses us from all sin." (NLT). His shining treasure permeates us with His light! How magnificent!

Personal Note:

I love candles, and especially votives that have a holder with cut out images so that the light can vividly glow through the image. That's what the Holy Spirit does with our lives. His light glows through the images of what Christ did on the cross for each of us personally, and pours through so that God does not see the cracks, only the image of His Son shining through our lives.

As I grow in Him, I realize that God needs my vessel to be totally broken before He can start the work of mending the cracks. Piece by piece, He picks me up with His marvelous fingers and starts healing me, one broken piece at a time. It has taken many years to heal all of the fractured damage of my vessel thus far, but God is patient beyond my imaginings, carefully and lovingly putting me back together. He is my healing balm. He is the mortar that cements my life. He alone can bring wholeness and completeness; but it is always my choice how much I allow Him to heal, control, and shine through me!

Prayer:

Oh Father, I bring before You the damaged jar of a life. Please take me in Your mighty hands and heal my wounds, crack-by-crack and piece-by-piece. Please help me to be willing to allow You to bring Your shining treasure, the Holy Spirit, to fill me with Your light that I may shine forth as a willing vessel in Your hands. In Jesus' name, Amen.

Your Reflections:

Day 42

God is . . . Like a Flowing River

Bible Reading: Isaiah 6:1-4

Worship, praise and thanksgiving are so closely related to God. They flow through our prayer time with Him like a river. Worship indicates an attitude of the heart or a posture of the body. In fact, the Jews when they worship move back and forth as they pray. They regard worship as both spiritual and physical. Praise has to do with utterance, either by mouth or by the heart. Praise is all about who He is! Thanksgiving is also an utterance, but it usually relates to what He has done.

When we are deep in His presence, His love returns to us from the flow of our worship; and the connection becomes like a river of adoration. We adore Him and He pours back into our hearts His matchless love, grace and mercy. It is a precious time that we can experience with our Lord and our God. Someday we will see God face to face and that will really be amazing worship!

Moses saw the back of God Almighty, but Isaiah saw the Lord. "I saw the Lord. He was sitting on a lofty throne, and the train of His robe filled the temple. Attending Him were mighty seraphim (angels), each having six wings. With two wings, they covered their faces, with two wings, they covered their feet and with two, they flew. They were calling out to each other, "Holy, holy, holy is the Lord of heaven's Armies! The whole earth is filled with His glory!" Isaiah 6:1b-3 (NLT).

Isaiah was so overwhelmed and frightened that he thought that he would die right there because he saw the Lord. I personally don't think that Isaiah actually saw God's face, because God had told Moses that no one could look upon His face and live. Even the seraphim that God created for worship cover their faces with two of their wings. Nevertheless, seeing as much of the Lord as he did, Isaiah felt so sinful in His presence. God sent a seraph down with a flaming coal to touch Isaiah's lips. "See, this coal has touched your lips. Now your guilt is removed and your sins are forgiven" Isaiah 6:7b (NLT). What a merciful God!

Personal Note:

We who were washed in the blood of Jesus are cleansed and our sins are removed forever and ever. Now we can have a river of adoration flowing between God and us! How phenomenal!

When I come to God in prayer all three of these things—worship, praise and thanksgiving—should flow smoothly to create this river of adoration. He sends back to me His love, mercy and grace and the river flows freely between God and man. As I become more comfortable with praying, with these three elements as center stage in my prayer, the flow comes freely and naturally sometimes with tears of gratitude and sometimes with a fullness in my heart that I cannot contain. Nevertheless, it is always with pure adoration to my Lord and my God. I always feel so honored to be in His presence and experience His river flowing freely from the throne of God!

Prayer:

O how I adore You, heavenly Father. I am so grateful to You that I have this kind of communion with You available to me. May I experience the river of adoration flowing freely through my spirit more and more often as I learn to please You. How astonishing You are in all Your ways. I worship You, through Jesus Christ my Lord, Amen.

Your Reflections:

Day 43

God is . . . Overflowing Joy

Bible Reading: Psalm 98:1-9

"Joy to the World the Lord is come. Let earth receive her King. Let every heart prepare Him room—and heaven and nature sing!" We sing this song often at Christmastime, but it really is all about our King of kings and Lord of lords! It fills my heart with overflowing joy. It has been just recently, however, that I've taken the time to truly understand the words "let heaven and nature sing." David knew how to rejoice with overflowing joy and praise to His God. "Shout joyful praises to God, all the earth! Sing about the glory of His name! Tell the world how glorious He is!"(NLT). That is how Psalm 66 begins.

When I think of praise and worship, I think of people raising their hands and voices in joyful praise. However, I never really thought about the earth being joyful. When I hear the wind whistling through the trees, do I stop and think that the wind and trees are making joyful praise to God? "Let the sea and everything in it shout His praise! Let the earth and all living things join in. Let the rivers clap their hands in glee! Let the hills sing out their songs of joy before the Lord" Psalm 98:7-9 (NLT).

I have always enjoyed a soft, gentle breeze blowing on my face. In addition, if I am very quiet, I can actually hear the music of the grasses blowing softly in the air. The picture that comes to mind is the wonderful musical, with Julie Andrews standing on top of the mountains, her hands outstretched, singing, "The Hills Are Alive with the Sound of Music."

We lived by a river and it was so peaceful and quiet there. We could hear the water gently moving over the rocks. Many times, I would sit on our deck and just listen to the silence. Do you know that silence is not real? There is always sound moving through something. All the earth is praising God, but much of what He hears is in a tone that we cannot hear. Isaiah 49:13 refers to the sounds that God hears. "Sing for joy, O heavens! Rejoice O earth! Burst into song, O mountains! For the Lord has comforted His people and will have compassion on them in their suffering" (NLT). Yes, all earth praises when God comforts us.

Jesus talked about how nature responds in praise. On the day we call Palm Sunday, He rode through the gates of Jerusalem on the back of a donkey. Everyone rejoiced and threw palm branches down to honor him. When the Pharisees started to rebuke the people, Jesus said, "I tell you . . . if they keep quiet, the stones will cry out" Luke 19:40 (NIV). How beautiful the sounds must be in heaven!

Personal Note:

I would love to know what the earth was like in the very beginning, when God created the heavens and the earth, as Adam and Eve walked in the garden in perfect harmony with creation and their Creator. I can only imagine how beautiful and vivid was every blossoming flower with its array of color, or how rich and vibrant each leaf on a tree appeared, and how green the grass must have been. However, way beyond that, how glorious the sounds of the earth were, with trees reaching upward to the sky to praise and glorify the God who made them all. We only get a glimpse of the wonder of our earth now; but someday, when we get to heaven, there is so much more awaiting us. I don't think my mortal body could stand it if I could see it now or my mind even comprehend it.

The next time I take a walk, or sit on the benches among the beautiful trees in our backyard amid God's nature, I am going to look a little deeper into the beauty around me. I am going to listen a little clearer and remember God's words to me in the Psalms, "Be still and know that I am God." It is in God's stillness that I find rest for my soul and comfort for my heart. Whenever He comforts me, I know that nature will burst out in joyful praise because the Creator of the Universe is comforting one of His children!

Prayer:

Oh, Father, thank you that Your joy is so full that it overflows into everything that You have made—You created the heavens and the earth for our pleasure and joy. Help me to appreciate Your blessing of nature more each day as I walk closer to You. In Jesus' name, Amen.

Your Reflections:

Day 44

God is . . . The Holy One

Bible Reading: Isaiah 43:1-10

It is so easy in the hustle and bustle of our everyday lives to forget who God really is. To make Him more accessible to us, we often demean Him without even thinking. Many times, we have the best of intentions, but we forget the very basis of God's attributes. God is holy. That is just who He is.

I think it would be interesting to e-mail or phone all our friends and ask, "If you had one adjective to describe me, what would it be?" My husband and I were talking one day and he said, "if you ever want to put anything on my tombstone put "P and P." Well, I got the first one very quickly. It was persistence. However, when he told me the second one, I knew it was also very true. It was patience. He was absolutely right. Those two attributes define him quite well. Throughout his life, those two attributes have been very consistent. (By the way, I am neither of those things. I come to the Lord all the time, asking especially for more patience),

When it comes to God, however, we try to change who He is by bringing Him down to our level. We often talk about His love for us, and that is great. However, we forget that His very nature is exalted far above anything that we can imagine. His holiness is His essence. Because of His holiness, we know that He is righteous, fair, loving and kind. We can depend upon Him always. "There is no other God, there never has been, and there never will be" Isaiah 43:10b (NLT). That is about as clear as Isaiah can put it.

God desperately wanted the children of Israel to remember His holiness. In Leviticus 11:44a He makes this statement, "For I am the Lord your God. You must consecrate yourselves and be holy, because

I am holy." (NLT). This was so important to Him that almost four books of the Bible are dedicated to the laws He set down to remind His people of His holiness.

Because Christ is our sacrificial Lamb who died for our sins, we no longer have to live by these rigid laws, but by the grace of our Lord Jesus Christ! "For God's will was for us to be made holy by the sacrifice of the body of Jesus Christ, once for all time" Hebrews 10:10 (NLT). Christ did it all for us. He was the ultimate sacrifice! "The Holy One," the Son of the living God!

Personal Note:

From my journal on May 8, 2000: "God by His very nature is holy, just as I am human. Realizing this fact is so awesome. It removes Him from merely being a benevolent Father with a long white beard who loves me "as long as I am good." It elevates Him to the One and only Almighty, all-powerful, holy one who loves me with a holy love."

We hear those around us who may not be aware of His holiness describing Him as "the man upstairs" or "big daddy." When I hear such statements, I know that person does not have any concept of who God really is! Now, because of all of the religious tolerance we are trying to identify Him as a "higher power." That is a step in the right direction. He really is—"The Highest Power!"—And I am so thankful that He is. The God of the universe with millions of galaxies looked down on this "dot" called earth and man who was smaller still, and said, "You are Mine and I want to be yours. I have given you free will, so that you can make your own choice. But I love you with an everlasting love and want you as part of My kingdom." I am really awed by that!

Prayer:

Thank you, Father, for Your holiness. Without it, You are diminished to my level. Your holiness and purity are so precious and You offer them to me as a way, or an example, of how I can experience Your true nature. Thank You that Jesus was willing to come and pay the price for my salvation that I might be holy in Your sight. In His mighty name, Amen.

Your Reflections:

Day 45

God is . . . Miraculously Merciful

Bible Reading: Exodus 15:22-26

Sometimes after a miraculous victory that is altogether God and not I, I go through my deepest valley. The Israelites experienced this as well. Talk about a miracle. In Exodus 15, they had just been celebrating and singing and were so jubilant after God brought them through the Red Sea. When the last Israelite stepped foot on dry ground, God released the sea and it swallowed up all of the Egyptians who were in hot pursuit to overtake the Israelites and bring them back to bondage in Egypt.

We began to see an immediate change as the Israelites started into the vast desert. "Then Moses led the people of Israel away from the Red Sea and they moved out into the desert of Shur" Exodus 15:22a (NLT). Three days into their journey, they found an oasis and were in dire need of water, but when they tasted the water, it was bitter. They named the place Marah, meaning bitter.

Did they remember the tremendous miracles that God had already performed in securing their freedom from Pharaoh? This was no easy feat, I might add. No! They not only complained but they turned against Moses. Therefore, Moses did the only thing that he knew to do—he cried out to the Lord. The Lord helped him immediately by directing him to a specific piece of wood. Moses threw it in the water and the water became drinkable. It does not say whether any of the people thanked God, or Moses, for yet another miracle, but before we become too hard on the Israelites, we might need to look inward.

How many times have we been on the mountaintop of blessing and then immediately entered the desert and started complaining? It is so human! As I grow in the Lord, He helps me to appreciate Him more; and as I am filled up with Him, I cannot be so filled up with myself. I am learning that obedience to Him is a far better way. The Psalmist wrote, "I long to obey your commandments! Renew my life with Your goodness" Psalm 119:40 (NLT). That is my heart's desire—to be obedient to His commands and filled up with His goodness, and then His miraculous mercy will flow freely into my life.

Personal Note:

In my spiritual journey, I have had many blessings and some real miracles. I think one of the major stepping-stones along my pathway was June 12, 2005. In January of that year, I had gone through a second arthroscopy surgery on my right knee. The MRI and x-rays showed that I had little or no cartilage in that knee. It was so painful that I could no longer walk on it for very long. I used a wheel chair for anything other than going just around the house and I used a crutch inside.

The surgery was not successful. Nevertheless, I was told that I was a good candidate for an orthopedic brace. I was measured, fitted, and started wearing the brace. I could walk a little better than before but not for a long period. At least I was able to give up the crutch, but I still used the wheel chair quite a bit because the brace was cumbersome and if I did not get it tight enough, there was slippage. The biggest improvement was that I could drive again.

On June 12, 2005, I was watching Dr. Charles Stanley on TV. He was preaching on "How to get direction through fasting and prayer." As I listened, I felt the Holy Spirit inside me say, "You need to fast and pray for your knee."

I had never done anything like that before. I had fasted before, on Good Friday and for other's needs, but not on a personal level. I called my daughter who I knew fasted quite often. She agreed with me and said that she wanted to fast with me. We set aside that Tuesday, June 14, 2005, as our day. I called many friends and asked them what requests they might have that I could bring before the Lord on that day as well.

By Tuesday, fewer than 48 hours after I had heard that sermon, I started fasting and praying. I was including 26 people in prayer on that special day. It was such an awesome experience and by 3:00 that afternoon, I was walking without help around the house. By that evening, you could not stop me. I am still walking with no assistance and as I am writing this, my right leg grows stronger every day!

It was a real turning point in my spiritual walk. Talk about a mountaintop experience! I wish I could say that I have never complained since that awesome day. I know that I still have times when I get grouchy or frustrated, but I have not forgotten my God who performs such mighty miracles. When I go into the valley of despair, my merciful Father is always there to remind me of His awesome power and strength.

Prayer:

Father, may I learn to appreciate, worship and praise You in hard times as well as good. You are the God of miracles and I only need turn to You and know that You are in complete control of all my needs and concerns. I thank You for dramatically healing my body. In Jesus' name, Amen.

Your Reflections:

Day 46

God is . . . Worthy of Honor

Bible Reading: Psalm 66:1-4

Honor is another way we can worship and praise the Lord, at least when we are talking about holy honor. David wrote, "Make a joyful shout to God, all the earth! Sing out the honor of His name, make His praise glorious" Psalm 66:1 (NKJ). When we are praying, praising and worshiping God, honor must be at the very core. We cannot really worship without it. "All the earth shall worship You and sing praises to You; they shall sing praises to Your name" Psalm 66:4 (NKJ).

Jesus taught us how to honor Him in prayer when He showed us the example of a Pharisee and a common publican praying. The Pharisee used big words and gestures and everything he did was so that he could be seen as such a "spiritual" man. The publican, on the other hand, bowed His head and his heart and said, "God, be merciful to me, a sinner" Luke 18:13b (NKJ). Christ said that the publican's prayer was heard by God and the Pharisee's was not. God looks on the inside and is the only one who can really know what we are like.

Another way to honor or dishonor God is by our actions. In I Samuel, we read of a priest named Eli. His sons were very wicked in God's sight. They would desecrate the sacrificial giving of the people and take whatever meat they wanted right off the sacrificial altar. "So the sin of these young men was very serious in the Lord's sight, for they treated the Lord's offerings with contempt" I Samuel 2:17 (NLT).

I cannot imagine us doing anything that disrespectful, but even though this is an extreme example, if we try to fit God into one of our "little boxes" so that He is a bit more human, we really are dishonoring Him and trying to make Him less than He is. "Who is like You among the gods, O Lord—glorious in holiness, awesome in splendor, performing great wonders?" Exodus 15:11 (NLT). Is He the God of the Universe who formed us, or is He just a god who will "bend the rules" for us? Are His holiness and honor important to us? That is the question.

Personal Note:

Rightly honoring God's holiness is the only way that I can truly respect Him. Jesus referred to prayer and honor more than once. "But when you pray, go into your room, close the door and pray to your Father, who is unseen. Then your Father, who sees what is done in secret, will reward you" Matthew 6:6 (NIV).

Having a special place set aside to honor my Father is nice, but the wonderful thing is that my heart is always secret to those around me. If I come to God with a sincere heart, He will bless me because He truly knows the intent of my heart. No matter whether I pray publicly or privately, when I come to Him in true adoration and gratitude for His holiness, He will honor my prayer and reward me!

Prayer:

Father, as I am learning so much more about You, please help me to always remember to come with an honorable heart in praise and worship to Your mighty name. In Jesus' name, Amen.

Your Reflections:

Day 47

God is . . . Our Standard of Morality

Bible Reading: 2 Corinthian 7:1-4

Morality is one area that I would avoid talking about if I could. Why is it so hard to talk about this virtue? It is because it sounds judgmental and in our society, we often do not have many moral laws in place. Webster defines morality as, "conformity to the rules of right conduct." What is right conduct? To know, we need to go to God's Word.

Paul speaks about this subject often to the young Christian church. Probably one of our more familiar passages would be in Romans. "And so dear brothers and sisters, I plead with you to give your bodies to God, because of all He has done for you. Let them be a living and holy sacrifice—the kind He will find acceptable. This is truly the way to worship Him. Don't copy the behavior and customs of this world, but let God transform you into a new person by changing the way you think. Then you will learn to know God's will for you, which is good and pleasing and perfect" Romans 12:1-2 (NLT).

WOW! That is powerful! The good news is that we do not have to figure out morality. God has done it for us! It is part of holiness! In his second letter to the Corinthians Paul writes, "Because we have these promises, dear friends, let us cleanse ourselves from everything that can defile our body or spirit. And let us work toward complete holiness because we fear God" 2 Corinthians 7:1 (NLT). There is no judgment here. In one Scripture, Paul calls us "dear brothers and sisters" and in the other one he says, "dear friends". Another thing I like about this last reading is that it tells us to work toward holiness.

None of us is perfect! We are all "works in progress," so we can be encouraged that as we learn to love our Lord more and imitate His behavior, we can come closer to holiness and morality! Jesus said,

"And I give myself as a holy sacrifice for them, so they can be made holy by Your truth" John 17:19 (NLT). Living holy upstanding moral lives has challenged people from the time of Adam and Eve, and our generation is no exception. As I allow God to work in me, He will bring about the changes that are not in line with His commands. What a wonderful God I serve!

Personal Note:

From my journal on May 5, 2000: "God wishes me above any other attribute to be holy. Leviticus 11:44 commands us to be holy. "I am the Lord Your God, consecrate yourselves and be holy, because I am holy" (NIV). I need to ask Him to cover us with His holiness, because reaching toward holiness will bring us closer to His goal for me.

In the world we live in today, where it seems so much more popular to "do my own thing," there really is no actual morality to grasp. This has been delegated to each family as they see fit. Nevertheless, God in His mercy has given me guidelines and commands to follow so that I can have the full, rich and rewarding life that He has planned for me. I am so grateful to be able to serve such a mighty God. My prayer is that I will become more holy and acceptable to Him each day. Praise be to God who gives me victory through His Name!

Prayer:

Thank you, Father, for giving me moral clarity through Your Word. Though I am far from perfect, You are the Maker of everything perfect. Because of Your Son's sacrifice, I can be holy and blameless before You. Mold me into Your purity as I learn to walk with you day by day. In Jesus' name, Amen.

Your Reflections:

Day 48

God is . . . My Temple Purifier

Bible Reading: I Corinthians 3:16-20

The temple has always been where God's holy presence lives. The first holy worship facility was the tabernacle which was a tent but made to specific dimensions. It included the inner chamber called the Holy of Holies. Only the high priest was allowed to go in there and then only once a year. Only after a very precise purification ritual was he presentable to go into the Holy of Holies as a representative of the people to God Almighty. He even had bells sewn into the hem of his garments; so that if God did not find him acceptable and the priests heard no movement, they would know God had struck him dead.

David wanted to build the first real temple to his God whom He loved so much, but God prevented him from doing so because David was a man of war. God promised to keep the land at peace; so that Solomon his son could take charge of having the first temple built, again with specific detailed directions from God. The Holy place and the Holy of Holies was still the manner that God continued to keep as a means of communicating through their high priest. The thing that separated these two areas was a special curtain that God Almighty designed.

These specific layout plans were strictly observed in the temple until Christ came and died on the cross. Then, "the curtain of the temple was torn in two from top to bottom" Mark 15:38 (NIV). This is very significant for all of Christ's followers, because He proclaimed on that day, that from then on, He alone would be the ultimate sacrifice for sin.

God's temple where He meets us and cleanses us today, is our inner being, our soul and spirit? The Bible calls it our heart. "Don't you realize that all of you together are the temple of God, and that the Spirit of God lives in you?" I Corinthians 3:16 (NLT). That is why it is so important that we continually ask God to purify our hearts and ask Him to show us areas where our temple is not pure, so that we can ask forgiveness of sin and He can purge that area from our lives. What an incredible sacrifice!

Personal Note:

From my journal on May 5, 2000: "The closer I walk with God and the more I get to know Him, the more I see my own inadequacy. His holiness, is so revealing that the nearer I get to Him the more I realize how far I have yet to go."

Isaiah felt so sinful when God revealed that wonderful vision of heaven and God on His throne. From a human point of view, Isaiah was a fine upstanding citizen, very well educated and probably from an aristocratic home. He was well respected and undoubtedly thought of as a very good man. Yet, next to God's holiness, Isaiah felt completely undone. "Then I said it's all over! I am doomed for I am a sinful man. I have filthy lips and I live among a people with filthy lips. Yet I have seen the King, the Lord of heaven's Armies" Isaiah 6:5 (NLT).

Coming before God's holiness, we all feel doomed. The good news is that Christ died and rose again, so that whenever God looks at us He looks through His perfect Son, therefore providing us with His perfection. No matter how unworthy I am, God lives in me through His Son. My part is to honor and adore Him and keep trusting Him to cleanse me, so that I may reach toward Christ's purity. Only His blood can cleanse this temple!

Prayer:

Oh Father, I am so in awe of You. To know that my body is Your temple is sobering. Make it pure and holy as I learn to allow You to purge my deep dark areas and continue to turn over my life to You. Thank You for Jesus who died that I might be Your temple, holy and acceptable to You. In His name, Amen.

Your Reflections:

Day 49

God is . . . Our Searcher of Hearts

Bible Reading: Jeremiah 17:7-10

We have talked about some direct subjects that all of us face as we grow in the Lord. I talked earlier about the prophet Isaiah who felt so insignificant in light of God's holiness. Even though He was a godly man, he felt very insignificant in the presence of the Almighty God.

I cannot even imagine literally seeing the throne of God and God sitting on it. When the Apostle John was a prisoner and exiled on the Island of Patmos, he was given the whole book of Revelation. He saw things that no other human has ever seen. John makes it very clear who the author was of this amazing book. "The revelation of Jesus Christ, which God gave Him to show His servants, what must soon take place. He made it known, by sending His angel to His servant John, who testifies to everything he saw . . . that is, the word of God and the testimony of Jesus Christ" Revelation 1:1-2 (NIV). It does not tell us how John felt when he saw all of this, but I am sure that he was humbled and awed to be in the presence of the Living God and to see Jesus again.

However, most of us do not feel like we could "hold a candle" to either of these godly men. God lets us know that none of us is perfect. Paul wrote, "All have sinned and fall short of the glory of God" Romans 3:23 (NIV). Not one of us could escape God's scrutiny if He judged us as we are, "works in progress." That is why Christ took our sin upon Himself so that we could come before a righteous and holy God, without sin or blame.

God knew that there would come a time when the offering up of sacrificial lambs would never be enough to cover us. Therefore, He did the unthinkable. In His great love, He sent His only Son to be born and live as a human, so that He could become the only sacrifice that would be good enough to cover our sin. In Romans, Paul wrote: "For God knew His people in advance, and He chose them to become like His Son, so that His Son would be the firstborn among many brothers and sisters" Romans 8:29 (NLT). What a plan! What a sacrifice! What extraordinary love God has for us! Once we accept Christ's sacrifice, God's radar searches our heart and sees only our Redeemer's purity and holiness.

Personal Note:

From my journal on May 17, 2000: "It is one thing to know that God is holy but it is quite another thing to come before that holiness with an open heart and ask Him to send His radar into the innermost corners of my heart and see me as I truly am."

Isaiah wrote, "all our righteousness is like filthy rags!" Isaiah 64:6b (KJV). But we can go from rags to riches, because of our Savior's sacrifice at Calvary. Sometimes I willingly let Him search and cleanse me. Other times, I let the cares and busyness of this life interfere, and the beam is not quite as bright. If I am not careful, it does not take much to replace His radar with the stresses of life. My prayer is to keep reaching out and opening up to Him, so that I may become filled with more of Him and less of me.

Prayer:

Oh Father, I pray that I will be willing for Your Spirit to search out all of the hidden areas of my heart. Examine me and cleanse every closed area that would prevent me from being all You want me to be. Thank You for Your wondrous love through Jesus Christ my Lord, Amen.

Your Reflections:

Day 50

God is . . . In the Thick Darkness

Bible Reading: Exodus 20:18-21

It had only been three months since God had so miraculously delivered the children of Israel out of the hands of slavery in Egypt and parted the Red Sea so that they could cross over safely and escape Pharaoh's Army. During this time there had been many complaints directed at Moses. The people murmured about how bad they had it and how much better it had been for them in Egypt.

Moses kept bringing their complaints to God and begging Him to forgive and provide and that is exactly what God did. He made bad water good and provided miraculous food, manna from heaven. Every morning the manna fell from heaven, except on the Sabbath. He guided and directed His people by a cloud by day and a fire by night!

In Exodus 19, we find that God wanted the people to understand completely that His hand was guiding Moses through every step they took. "Behold, I come to you in the thick cloud, that the people may hear what I speak with you, and believe you forever" Exodus 19:9a (NKJ). God spoke directly to Moses, telling the people to sanctify themselves and then come to the base of the mountain. They were not to touch the mountain because it was holy and they would die.

Moses paints a picture of a God so powerful that it is frightening. "Now all the people witnessed the thundering, the lightening flashes, the sound of the trumpet and the mountain smoking and when the people saw it they trembled." However, verse 21 is what was very interesting. "So the people stood afar off, but Moses drew near the ***thick darkness*** where God was" Exodus 20:18,21 (NKJ). *(emphasis mine)*. It was at this time that God personally wrote the Ten Commandments with His finger, as well as giving Moses all of the laws for the people to live by.

Personal Note:

Sometimes, we have to go into the thick darkness to meet God before He can bring us farther up the mountain toward His glory. I had not really seen this verse in that way before. This was such a marvelous revelation to me as I was having a personal struggle and was praying for direction. My spirit was heavy and I asked God to show me what He wanted me to read today. I had finished my usual Bible reading and was not sure where to go next. I was drawn to read about Moses and the glory of God. I was so overwhelmed by God's presence that I could not speak, or write, or do anything but praise Him for nearly an hour. I missed going to church, but somehow, I felt that it was more than all right!

There were times in my writing where God changed the devotional note title that I had prepared and I had not even checked my notes to see what title I was going to be writing about this particular day. As I started to replace what I originally wrote with this new concept, there were my notes written in May of 2000 about Moses on Mt Sinai, asking God to show him His glory! I was shaken by the power of God leading my life.

I also had listened to a sermon earlier that morning, about how God speaks to us through Scripture. Dr. Stanley again! It seems that the Lord is really using him in my life. What he said was that as we meditate on God's word, there are times when something just practically "jumps off the page." This is one of the ways God speaks to us. Lo and behold, a short time later, the Scripture highlighted in my notes just jumped off the page and God's presence was so awesome. I am still in awe of what He performed in me that day, and so humbled and grateful!

Prayer:

Father, I thank you that You still speak to me today in many ways. I come humbly before You to guide and direct me. Sometimes I must go through the thick darkness where You are, before I reach the brilliance of Your majesty and glory! Thank You for working so personally through my life. In Jesus' name, Amen.

Your Reflections:

Day 51

God is . . . Wealthy with Grace

Bible Reading: Ephesians 2:4-10

A little girl watched her great-grandparents pull dollar bills from between the pages of a gift book at their 60th wedding anniversary celebration. Wide-eyed with wonder she exclaimed, "You guys are rich!" Even if those bills had added up to sixty million dollars, they could not begin to compare to the wealth of God's riches in mercy and grace toward His children.

When I think of God's wealth, I usually think of Malachi 3:10 (NLT). "I will open the windows of heaven for you. I will pour out a blessing so great you won't have enough room to take it in." What is behind those windows of heaven? I think of a bright sunny day with the light of the sun bathing every nook and cranny of my heart, filling me with the warmth of His grace, mercy, provision and blessing. Right when my heart is full and spilling over He continues to pour, filling my soul, my spirit, and my body until I am so saturated that I am overflowing with His abundance.

God has always shown mercy abundantly throughout the ages. He has proven His great love and grace repeatedly when His chosen people rejected Him and served the other gods of the land. We read of miracle after miracle that He performed on behalf of His people. Moreover, He often used His prophets to bring His people back to Him. We see His grace displayed clearly, from the time that Moses freed them from bondage in Egypt, throughout the years of the judges, and then through all of the kings in both Israel and Judah.

The God of the universe loves us so much that He has provided a wealth of grace for us. What do we have to do in return? All we need to do is accept His Son and the sacrifice that He made for us when

He died on the cross. "So God can point to us in all future ages as examples of the incredible wealth of His grace and kindness toward us as shown in all that He has done for us who are united with Christ Jesus" Ephesians 2:7 (NLT). How I praise Him for His rich grace, which He bestows on me every day!

Personal Note:

I love the Scripture for today's reading. "But God is so rich in mercy, and He loves us so much, that even though we were dead because of our sin, He gave us life when He raised Christ from the dead. It is only by God's grace that you have been saved. For He raised us from the dead along with Christ and seated us with Him in the heavenly realms, because we are united with Christ Jesus" Ephesians 2:4-6 (NLT). When my Father does something, it is always huge. There can never be any doubt that it is our Almighty God doing it! How amazing is the wealth of His grace for me!

Prayer:

Father, how I love You. I can never begin to thank You for the wealth of Your grace. My heart is overwhelmed with adoration and gratitude. To try to comprehend what Christ did for me is beyond me. Nevertheless, I accept Your matchless gift and thank You. In Jesus' name, Amen.

Your Reflections:

Day 52

God is . . . The Exonerator

Bible Reading: Isaiah 53:7-11

What does it mean to be exonerated from something? Imagine the worst serial killer on trial. As he faces the judge, a man steps in front of him and overshadows him so that the judge can no longer see the murderer. All of the court's wrath and the death penalty are put on the man shielding the killer. After the sentence is pronounced, the man turns to the murderer with eyes of nothing but love and forgiveness and says, "I have paid your penalty. You are free to go! You are completely set free inside and out so that you never will have to commit another heinous crime. I exonerate you!"

That is what the love of God did through His Son Jesus. Isaiah 53 is one of my favorite passages about the Lamb of God. I read this passage quite often. Verse 7 reads, "He was led like a lamb to the slaughter and as a sheep before her shearer's is silent, so He did not open His mouth." Verse 12 ends with, "Therefore I will give Him a portion among the great, and He will divide the spoils with the strong. because He poured out His life unto death, and was numbered with the transgressors. For He bore the sin of many, and made intercession for the transgressors" (NIV). Yes, God did more than just forgive our sins. He completely exonerated us! Through Jesus, we share in His inheritance and every honor that is bestowed on Him as well. We are now counted as His descendants. Therefore, when we are filling out our family tree, we are in the direct line of the King of Kings and Lord of Lords. We are royalty in the truest sense.

When we try to forgive someone, as mere mortals, it is very hard to forget the deed as well. However, not our heavenly Father, who said "I—Yes, I alone—will blot out your sins for my own sake, and will never think of them again" Isaiah 43:25 (NLT). Talk about exoneration! He is beyond our human understanding!

Personal Note:

I think that being able to forgive another for a deep hurt is one of our biggest challenges. When I even try to think of the difference between God forgiving and me forgiving, I feel so inadequate—and I am! God knows that it is humanly impossible for me to exonerate others. Jesus commanded us to forgive, so we must, if we want to be obedient to Him.

He would never leave me out on a limb with no rescue in sight. It is only through His grace that I can find forgiveness from Him for my transgressions, but also through Him, so that I am able to forgive others. It is dying to self and turning it over to Him that will help me forgive others more readily. Sometimes the hurt is so deep that it takes time. Nevertheless, God is always patient to forgive my weaknesses and He says that His strength is made perfect in my weakness.

Forgiving others is both the easiest way to heal from the hurt and the hardest to do. Only when I can turn things fully over to my healer, Jesus Christ, and let Him carry the hurt and heal me, can I then start to forgive as Christ forgives me.

Prayer:

Father, thank You for being so forgiving that You exonerate me from every sin. Such forgiveness can only be accomplished through the sacrifice of Your Lamb who shed His blood for the remission of our sin. I praise You and adore You. In my Redeemer's name, Amen.

Your Reflections:

Day 53

God is . . . A Team Coach

Bible Reading: Acts 1:15-18

God has always been a Team Coach. He could have taken His creation of man in any direction that He wanted. After all, He made us! Nevertheless, His greatest desire was to use us, by our own choice, as part of His team. Many times, probably most of the time, He had only one player on His team at one time. Still that one person used in the hands of God often affected many lives and, sometimes, all mankind. His rules were always the same: "Let me mold you and make you into the player that I know you can be."

The rules changed a bit when Jesus came to earth. From that day forward, God had a bigger and bigger team of willing players. One of the first things Jesus did, at the beginning of His ministry, was to choose a team. He handpicked each one and that twelve-man team was with Him throughout His three-and-a-half year ministry. He knew each of His players and all of the variables of their personalities and backgrounds. He also knew the future and what impact each of them would have on history.

We will take a closer look at the one man who did not want to play ball according to God's rules. Judas Iscariot was a very important part of the team. He sat under the same Jesus as the other eleven, saw the same miracles, and heard the same teaching. However, after being with the team for that long, Judas finally decided that Jesus was not the One he thought He was, so he became a free agent and tried to play ball with the Pharisees. That was the worst decision he ever made, but he realized, too late, that he had made a mistake.

After such a betrayal, would Jesus have taken him back? Of course, He would have, but Judas was so full of guilt and remorse that he committed suicide.

Although Jesus knew that Judas would make this horrible decision when He asked Him to be His disciple, Judas had many opportunities to change his mind. I believe that Judas had a struggle between humbling himself and asking the Lord for forgiveness, and the choice that he ended up making. I believe this, because we always have the choice between serving the Lord and serving Satan. The only difference between Judas and us is that he made the wrong choice.

In Acts, it tells us how Peter stood up in front of the 120 members of the very first church and said, "Brothers, the scripture had to be fulfilled concerning Judas, who guided those who arrested Jesus. This was predicted long ago, by the Holy Spirit speaking through King David. Judas was one of us, and shared in the ministry with us" Acts 1:16,17 (NLT). David predicts this in Psalm 41: "Even my best friend, the one I trusted completely, the one who shared my food, has turned against me" Psalm 41:9 (NLT). Peter was a wonderful example to the first church. Peter, who himself had turned His back on Christ, may have understood Judas better than any of the other disciples. The difference between these two men was their choice. One asked for forgiveness and was fully forgiven; the other went down to his grave with his guilt and remorse.

Personal Note:

Choice is the whole issue. What will my team be? I am glad that I made the decision to be on the Lord's team! That is only the beginning, however. Day by day, hour by hour, His grace is poured out to me. Each day when I wake up in the morning, I have a new choice. Do I want to be on God's team today, or do I want to try to be a free agent? We are only truly free when we are completely in God's hands.

God's team is always the winning team. However, it is not always the easiest one to choose. It is my very nature to want to be in control of my life. God's best is for me to allow Him to be in control of my life. Therefore, the struggle goes on. Nevertheless, each step that I take toward Him is a step in the right direction.

Prayer:

Father, I thank You that You want me to be a team player. You alone can lead me into righteousness and blessing. Please help me to allow You to lead me in Your plan for me. In Jesus' name I pray, Amen.

Your Reflections:

Day 54

God is . . . My Seal of Authority

Bible Reading: Haggai 2:20-23

Haggai is one of the minor prophets. Minor refers to the size of the books of the Bible, not to the size of the prophet. The book is only two chapters long, but it is a little gem nestled among giants. Haggai's message is clear, easy to read, and very relevant for us today. It is all about values, priorities and what is on our "to do" list. The people had finally been free from exile in Babylon and in 538 B.C., King Cyrus allowed the people to return to their beloved city of Jerusalem to rebuild their temple.

At first, this was an exciting prospect, however, zeal waned and apathy began to set in. By 530 B.C., the work on the temple came to a screeching halt. The people began to let other priorities fill in; and soon they were not thinking at all about the temple and what they were set free to accomplish. They had their own homes to build, families to raise and business pressures closing in. Therefore, God was put on the "back burner."

That is when God intervened once again. He called a prophet named Haggai, the first to be sent by God since the return from exile. He was an encourager. He wanted to light a fire under the people and help them realize that their priorities had been turned upside down. Haggai told the people, in essence, that they were spending all of their time working to build bigger houses, crops and businesses, but all of their efforts were useless, because God wanted them to place their priorities and skills on building His house the Temple, not on themselves.

The Governor of Judah, Zerubbabel, heard the message loud and clear and helped rally the people who became excited once again to work on God's temple. I am encouraged when I read this short book, because it is so relevant for us today. It reminds us that God's work should still be our number one priority, even among our busyness and stresses.

In the very last verse in the book of Haggai, the words are spoken to the Governor. "But when this happens, says the Lord of Heaven's Armies, I will honor you, Zerubbabel . . . my servant, I will make you like a signet ring on my finger" Haggai 2:23a (NLT). The signet ring was a permanent seal that kings used to make a decree or document irrefutable. Once the seal or signet was stamped on the document, even the king himself could not go back on the decree without losing face. It literally sealed the contract. Can we even imagine what it was like for the governor of Judah to have God's seal of authority stamped on the pages of history—because he followed God's plans?

Personal Note:

Priorities are one of my biggest challenges! My desire is to have God and His plan take first place in my life. Do I always accomplish this? No! However, it happens more often than in the past! I have to say that as I have asked my Father to show me His plan and guide my life, and then really trust Him to do so, He has never failed.

No matter where I am on my journey with Him, there are distractions along the way. We all need encouragement and nudging from time to time. When I get too rushed or busy, I turn to Him more often and more quickly than I did before. I have my moments, however, when I pull away a little from my Lord. That is when He puts something in my path to remind me that I need to come back, take Him by the hand and let Him be my top priority once again. My heart's desire is to have God's signet ring of approval stamped on my life. I pray that in my busyness I will hear His gentle nudges, so that He does not have to send a "shout" in my direction.

Prayer:

Father, thank You for being available to help me draw closer to You. There is nothing more important than fulfilling Your purpose for me. Help me to remember that Your seal of authority is stamped forever on my life, because of Jesus! In my Savior's name, Amen.

Your Reflections:

Day 55

God is . . . The Great Commissioner

Bible Reading: Isaiah 6:8-13

Many of us, when we look at this title, would be reminded of the "great commission" that Christ gave as He was ascending into heaven, but I want to look at it with a little different perspective.

When Isaiah, the prophet saw the vision of God on His throne, he was asked a specific question by God. In verse 8, he wrote, "Then I heard the Lord asking, whom shall I send as a messenger to this people? Who will go for us?" (NLT), Isaiah's response was immediate. "Here am I, send me!" God did not force this on Isaiah, or try to railroad him into doing this. It sounds more like a partnership.

I think Isaiah had this spectacular vision, because God had an unusual commission to give him. Usually God calls us to spread the good news of salvation and repentance, but this one was different. God told Isaiah, "Make the heart of this people calloused, make their ears dull and close their eyes. Then Isaiah asked, "For how long O Lord?" and God answered, "Until the cities lie ruined and without inhabitants, until the houses are left deserted, and the fields ruined and ravished" Isaiah 6:10a,11 (NIV).

How confused Isaiah must have been. Nevertheless, he had seen what no one else had ever seen—the mighty God in Heaven sitting upon His throne. After such a vision, Isaiah was not in any position to argue with his God. I can't help but wonder, without this magnificent vision would Isaiah have been so willing to bring such a message to the people? However, the people had hardened their hearts so much by that time that God knew they would not respond to His love and mercy. His patience was starting to wane and judgment was fast approaching.

The people would have to be exiled before they would be able to serve the true and living God again, but God always has those who will never forsake Him. "A remnant will return, yes, the remnant of Jacob will return to the Mighty God" Isaiah 10:21 (NLT). There will always be the faithful few! That is God's promise!

Personal Note:

I do not like confrontation. I would rather "go with the flow" than have to confront anyone. I have grown in this area, but I wonder, would I have been able to bring such a message if God had called me? Is it really that much different today?

Though God's message sounded different, it really was the same. It was the people's attitudes toward what He said that had changed so much. Isaiah was only asked to preach the message of repentance or destruction. It was up to the people to accept or reject it. Unfortunately, only a remnant responded to God's call, as only a few people today respond to His call. The world goes around and around, but history proves that nothing really changes until God grabs hold of our heartstrings and we yield our lives to our Great Commissioner, the God of the universe! Where are we in America today? Are we close to having God's judgment fall on us?

Prayer:

O Father, You have been so merciful to us as a country and You have blessed us abundantly. I am so thankful that You temper justice with mercy. Lord, help me to serve You faithfully and be willing to fulfill Your purpose for me: to be counted among the faithful. In Jesus' name I pray, Amen.

Your Reflections:

Day 56

God is . . . A Ray of Hope

Bible Reading: Psalm 16:1-8

I will never forget the day that our daughter Jill was diagnosed with a catastrophic disease at age 16. Our entire world came crashing down upon us. Our beautiful daughter who was destined for greatness would only have six months to live. She would not see graduation from high school, never get married or have children. "Father, it is too soon for her life to end," I cried!

Those were extremely dark days for our family. We set up appointments with specialists. Finally, she went to one specialist who was much more familiar with her symptoms. It would not be as bad as we first thought. Although she would suffer with a chronic disease, Lupus, she could learn to manage that and, if God willed it, live a fruitful life, even though it would be a very difficult one.

It is in times such as these that our Father can be our only ray of hope as we wend our way through the rocky slopes and deep valleys of life, and feel the darkness close in.

It is likely the disciples felt this way when Jesus was arrested. They thought that they had lost their one ray of hope. Jesus, the One they felt was the true Messiah, was arrested. All kinds of false statements were being thrown about. What were they to do now? They had been with Him for over three years. With all of the miracles that He performed right before their eyes, the teachings, and His talking about how He and the Father were One, surely, He was the Promised One. What was happening? This was not the plan they thought He would use. They were so confused! They scattered and then they met up in a very private place, hunkering down and waiting—for what?

When they found out that He was going to be crucified, John and some of the women, including Jesus' mother and Mary Magdalene, decided they must go to where He was being executed. They had to know! Would He come down off the cross and save Himself? Then, from the cross came the instructions to John. "John, take care of my mother. She is now your mother. Mother, you are to go with John now. He will take care of you." Had their last ray of hope been dashed?

Then came that bright and glorious morning, the first day of the week! Jesus rose from the dead! When He came and showed Himself to all of the disciples, they were filled with awe and wonder at the stunning events of that radiant morning. Their hopes had not died on the cross. Jesus had risen from the grave! He was with them for 40 days, teaching and talking with them. "When the Lord Jesus had finished talking with them, He was taken up into heaven and sat down in the place of honor at God's right hand" Mark 16:19 (NLT). Jesus was their Ray of Hope, their future. Their lives were changed forever and so was the course of history!

Personal Note:

All through the Old Testament, God always had a last ray of hope for His children. He always had someone who could come before Him, on the people's behalf, and try to bring them back into His design for them. After 400 years of silence, God sent His beloved Son. Jesus who was more, much more than a ray of hope. His resurrection brought with it a "Glorious Hope" that we now have new life because of Him. What a blessing!

Prayer:

Oh Father, thank You for always giving me a ray of hope. I thank You especially for my Redeemer's resurrection that brought me into a completely new level of hope. I praise You for sending Your Son to die for my sins. In His name I pray, Amen.

Your Reflections:

Day 57

God is . . . The Ultimate Choice

Bible Reading: Romans 11:1-5

Choices! We make them every day. What will we eat? What will we wear? Yes, these are small, and maybe insignificant when it comes to the overall picture of our life, but still we understand on the minutest level, the concept of choice.

Yet, because God is so vast and complicated as far as our understanding goes, we cannot comprehend how He chooses us. Why would a just God create all humanity knowing before He did it, that some would come into His family and love Him and some would never make the decision to believe in Him?

When a potter gets a piece of clay in His hands and starts to mold it, sometimes it becomes something delicate and beautiful for all to behold. However, at other times, no matter how He tries to mold it into something beautiful, it seems to have a life of its own and is unusable. When that happens, even though he has given it every opportunity for greatness, he must let it go and cast it away.

God talks a lot about His choices. In today's reading, Paul is explaining some of how God thinks. "No, God has not rejected His own people whom He chose from the very beginning. Do you realize what the Scriptures say about this? Elijah the prophet complained to God about the people of Israel and said; 'Lord, they have killed Your prophets and torn down Your altars. I am the only one left, and now they are trying to kill me, too. Do you remember God's reply? He said 'No, Elijah, I have 7000 others who have never bowed down to Baal!" Romans 11:2-4 (NLT).

God always knows everything about us. He knows that we are all sinners, but He loves us and continues to try to save us. "The Lord is not slow in keeping His promise, as some understand slowness. He is patient with you, not wanting anyone to perish, but everyone to come into repentance" 2 Peter 3:9 (NIV). Yes, when we accept this gift, how wonderful it is for those of us who believe on His name and have become His chosen ones! Since Christ died on the cross and paid the penalty for our sins, God's chosen ones include not only Israel, but also every person in every nation of every color around the whole world. It is very precious to Him when one lost soul comes into His kingdom!

Personal Note:

From my journal on June 21, 2000: "God is the One who knows the ultimate fate of humankind. He knows our hearts. He alone knows how deep our rebellion is against the Truth or how open we are to His Word. He is a just God and He knows how tender or tough our hearts can be. It is not God's will that anyone should perish but that everyone should come to Him. However, the stubbornness of man prevents that from happening. Just like Adam and Eve in the garden, we are all given the choice—to choose God's plan or to turn our backs on Him." That is the Ultimate Choice!

Prayer:

Father, I am so glad that You chose me long before I was even born. Help me to yield to Your molding hands and become more of what You fashioned me to be. I thank You that I am part of Your kingdom. In Christ's name, Amen.

Your Reflections:

Day 58

God is . . . Our Adoptive Father

Bible Reading: Romans 8:5-16

Adopting a child today can be a long and tedious process. Many of us know of someone who has done this, or at least know a little about the procedures that we would go through, to adopt a child into our homes. It is never an easy course of action, but some adoptions are easier than others are.

A friend of mine just adopted a special-needs child last year. It was agony for her, because she is a single parent and has been in the foster care system for many years. She is an exceptional person and such a blessing to me. Her only daughter became a paraplegic when she was twelve. Laila is now in her twenties. Claire knew all about caring for special needs children.

She also started taking care of newborn drug-addicted babies and they became very close to her heart. Claire has never forgotten any child who has been blessed to come under her roof. She has pictures of each one and still remembers all of their birthdays. When this special little girl came to her, she knew that this child needed her as much as she needed Chandy. She was on the roller coaster of red tape for nearly two years. We prayed many times that God would grant her desire and break through all of the hoops that needed to be jumped through, before this child would be legally hers. What a day of rejoicing when Chandy was finally hers!

You would think since God created us, that it would be easy for Him to claim us as His own forever. Nevertheless, that was not the case. It took the ultimate sacrifice of God giving up His only Son to come to earth to die for us, before He could declare that we are His own. Even then, God loves us with a love that no human parent can even imagine, He still cannot claim us as His own unless we are willing to accept His Son's sacrifice. If we do not receive His Son, then he cannot accept us. It is that simple, yet heartbreaking, for our loving God.

"And we know that God causes everything to work together for the good of those that love God and are called according to His purpose for them. For God knew His people in advance, and He chose them to become like His Son, so that His Son would be the firstborn among many brothers and sisters" Romans 8:28-29 (NLT).

Personal Note:

I have read this passage in Romans countless times but the impact of Jesus, as my brother never hit me, until several months ago when I was having quiet time with my Father. I was sitting there just praying and praising, when all of a sudden, the picture came to mind of Jesus reaching out to me like a brother. You see, I had three sisters, (one is still living), but I never had a brother; so this beautiful picture was another one of God's many gifts to me as His child and Christ's sister. What a Brother my heavenly Father gave to me!

My son, Chris, and daughter-in-law, Kim, are starting through the adoption process so that my only grandson, (their only child) may have a brother or sister. They are wonderful parents. How we rejoice with them and pray that the process will go smoothly for them. God knows how important it is to have brothers and sisters. Therefore, even though we are not all blessed here on earth to have them, God wants to make sure that His Son has brothers and sisters. Therefore, our Savior and Redeemer is also our big Brother. How awesome! How extraordinary! How like our Father!

Prayer:

Father, how grateful I am that You love me and want me to be Your own child. How I thank You for sending Jesus to pay the adoption price for me, making me a part of Your divine family. I thank You, my Brother, my precious Redeemer, for Your sacrifice. How I am awed by You! In Your precious name, Amen.

Your Reflections:

Day 59

God is . . . Our Rich Inheritance

Bible Reading: Hebrews 9:24-28

I have not personally been in a family which had to bring together all of the relatives of a wealthy person who died and left a will. In many ways, I am glad that I do not have to worry about an inheritance because in some cases individuals take each other to court, or fight, and never speak to one another again. Unfortunately, this is more common than we might think.

However, in God's kingdom it is quite different. All that is required to become one of His heirs is accept His Son as the only sacrifice for our sins. In the Old Testament, the only way that people could come before a righteous and Holy God was to bring a sin offering. That was often a lamb; and by bringing this sacrifice before God, the spilled blood would cleanse them from their sins.

It was quite a ritual. Moreover, it was given to the Israelites so that they would be very clear about God's plan for them. It was the only way they could ever hope to be forgiven for their sins. Then God sent His Son to earth to become a sacrifice of atonement for sin. God knew that the only way we could partake of His rich inheritance was for Jesus to become a human and live a perfect, pure and holy life. Then He must die; and by shedding His blood, He could be our sacrifice to God, once and for all!

"That is why Jesus is the One who mediates a new covenant between God and people, so that all who are called can receive the eternal inheritance God has promised to them" Hebrews 9:15 (NLT). When we accept what Jesus did for us, we are now fully forgiven forever, and we become a part of God's lavish and luxurious kingdom. The riches He has for us are beyond our most elaborate imaginings.

What an amazingly rich inheritance we have through Jesus! What an indescribable kingdom we are a part of forever!

Personal Note:

When our two granddaughters, Michelle and Melissa, came to our house to visit, I remember them playing princess or "dress up." They would don all of my fancy clothes and jewelry. With eyes shining and spirits soaring, they came and showed my daughter, Jill and me, how beautiful and special they were. Oh, what fun they had!

I can only imagine what it will be like when Christ comes back and takes His bride home. What beautiful garments we will be given! Our loved ones, and all those who have gone on before us, will rise from their graves and meet us in the air. Oh, what a reception!

Then God will prepare a feast and we will sit down as a family and partake of all of His riches. I cannot even imagine what will be prepared for us. He will place crowns on our heads and we will be given rewards for our faithfulness here on earth. We will be royalty in the grandest sense. Our Prince, the King of kings and Lord of lords, will have come for us. His Majesty, Jesus Christ, our King in shining armor! What a glorious and spectacular day that will be.

Prayer:

Father, because You love us so much, You sent Your only Son to make atonement for us. In so doing, we have become heirs with Christ in Your Kingdom. I thank You for personally including me. I feel so humbled by your sacrifice. In Jesus' name, Amen.

Your Reflections:

Day 60

God is . . . Sure-footed

Bible Reading: Habakkuk 3:17-19

Today we have paved roadways and sidewalks that we can walk on, but it was not always so. When I was a little girl, I often walked on unstable ground. Some dirt paths all of a sudden would produce a rock or a pothole, and I would lose my footing. I seldom watched where I was going, anywhere, and I was always barefooted. I ran ahead of my mother and loved to pick wild flowers, a pretty rock or anything that would catch my eye as I went merrily on my path. There was an adventure in every step, so it was easy for me to misjudge my footing. I remember my mother scolding me and saying, "Clarice, you must watch where you walk."

Our Christian walk is just like that. God has a lot to say about our path and our feet. "Surely God is good to Israel, to those who are pure in heart. But as for me, my feet had almost slipped; I had nearly lost my foothold" Psalm 73:1-2 (NIV).

Asaph, the chief musician who wrote that psalm, knew that in this life he would have struggles. He would not always feel like he was on solid ground. However, God gave us a clear picture of how to make sure we are on solid ground. "I waited patiently for the Lord to help me, and He turned to me and heard my cry. He lifted me out of the pit of despair, out of the mud and the mire. He set my feet on solid ground and steadied me as I walked along" Psalm 40:1-3 (NLT).

My impatient nature does not always want to wait on God to lift me and place me on solid ground. I want to run on ahead of Him and when I do, I usually stumble. Then He lifts me back up and places me upon His solid ground again.

Whenever we let Him, He makes us surefooted. Habakkuk wrote this wonderful truth. "The Sovereign Lord is my strength! He makes me as surefooted as a deer, able to tread upon the heights" Habakkuk 3:19 (NLT).

Personal Note:

When my husband was in his thirties he was touring the plant where he worked, and the heel of his shoe got caught in one of the wooden blocks of the flooring causing his right ankle to be torn up. While recuperating at home, his crutches slipped out from under him on our tile entryway resulting in him severely injuring the other ankle. There he was literally "without a leg to stand on." His prognosis was not good. They said that it was very probable that rheumatoid arthritis would set in and that he might never walk normally again.

Don faced many challenges during the months of his recuperation. It was hard for him to pray about it, but the Lord never forgot him, even in his darkest hours. God gave a special Scripture to him that has been his mainstay ever since. "So tighten your loosening grip and steady your wavering stand. Don't wander away from the path but forge steadily onward. On the right path the limping foot recovers strength and does not collapse" Hebrews 12:13 (Phillips translation). Through much prayer, patience, and perseverance, he regained about 95% use of his ankles and was able to continue His career. God will never fail us when we let him keep us sure-footed!

Prayer:

Thank You, Father, for keeping me on solid ground. Only You can make my feet steady as I follow You along Your path for me. Help me not to forget that my grounding is in You. You alone can make me sure-footed. In Jesus' name, Amen.

Your Reflections:

Day 61

God is . . . Supreme Timing

Bible Reading: Habakkuk 1:1-4

When Don and I first moved to Oregon from the Bay Area in California, the local television news was so refreshing. We would hear, perhaps, about a cow getting stuck in the mud or a new store opening, instead of the horrible news we were used to hearing in the Bay Area. Today, however, we cannot turn on the news or read a newspaper without reading about a horrible murder or rape or some other violent act. We live in a world where we have no security in knowing if some horrendous terror attack will hit our country again. Every day we are faced with more violence in the never-ending wars around the world. We want to ask like Habakkuk, "How long, Lord, will these things go on?"

Habakkuk's ministry as a prophet started around 612 B.C. He was a prophet of Judah right before the Babylonian Empire took God's people into captivity. The questions he asked of God would strike a cord with anyone concerned about the environment in which we live today. He asked, "How long, O Lord, must I call for help, but You do not listen? Or cry out to You, Violence! But You do not save? Why do you make me look at injustice? Why do You tolerate wrong? Destruction and violence are before me; there is strife, and conflict abounds. Therefore, the law is paralyzed, and justice never prevails. The wicked hem in the righteous, so that justice is perverted" Habakkuk 1:2-4 (NIV).

Does this sound familiar? He could have been writing this today, right here in our own country! His ministry ended in 589 B.C., and just three years later in 586 B.C., Judah fell and Jerusalem was destroyed.

God's timing is always perfect. It has little or nothing to do with our timing. Even though wickedness abounded greatly, God still saw a tiny spark left in His chosen people; and even though they were captives of Babylon, He mercifully brought them back to His beloved city one more time. But they had to go through His judgment time first. The Lord said, "'Come! Come! Flee from the land of the north . . . for I have scattered you to the four winds of heaven,' declares the Lord. 'Come, O Zion! Escape, you who live in the Daughter of Babylon!'" Zechariah 2:6-7 (NIV.) Israel's struggle is still currently going on. Nevertheless, God knows the exact time that He will again bring peace to Israel.

Personal Note:

We are not much different today. God sent His Son to be the ultimate sacrifice for our sins. For those of us who accept His sacrifice He brings so much love and assurance. We know that we will look forward someday to joining Him in His kingdom.

However, some who do not believe in Him are performing the most horrific kinds of acts against Him. We can almost hear Habakkuk's questions ringing in our own ears! "How long, Lord, How long?" However, it is not our timing to know how long and how patient our Father is. We think a century is a long time and it is, for us. But if we take a quick step back to look at our world a century ago and compare it to our world today, we can quickly see the degradation and lack of respect for God.

"How can He let this go on any longer?" we may ask. Only God in His sovereignty knows His timing. At the right time, God will send his Son back to earth; and then the violence will end and we will have a thousand years of peace. That is something that none of us has ever experienced in our lifetime! I am looking forward to this with great anticipation. How wonderful God's timing is!

Prayer:

Father, I cannot understand Your timing. Nevertheless, I am so thankful that You control everything that goes on. Even when things look bleak, I can trust You. Everything happens according to Your perfect purpose and by Your Divine permission. You are awesome beyond words! Thank You! In Jesus' name, Amen.

Your Reflections:

Day 62

God is . . . A Clarifier of Confusion

Bible Reading: I Samuel 16:6-12

Frequently in my life, I have been confused about my spiritual direction. Many times I have wandered aimlessly just waiting to figure out what God wanted me to do. Last year was one of those years. I just could not figure out how He could possibly use me, at my age. What did He want me to do? It was a real period of soul searching and tremendous spiritual growth.

There are many examples throughout Scripture regarding how God uses His people to perform things in ways different from the prophet or servant was expecting. One example was when God told Samuel to go and anoint one of the sons of Jesse as king.

Samuel had been the one to anoint Saul as the first king of Israel and even though Saul had turned against God's commands, Samuel still had a soft spot in his heart for him.

In today's reading, we find that God sent Samuel to a man named Jesse and told him to bring his sons before him, because God wanted to anoint one of them as Israel's next king. Samuel was impressed with Eliab, the first son. He was everything that you would think of as kingly—tall, stately and handsome! Nevertheless, God told Samuel in verse 7, "Don't judge by his appearance or height, for I have rejected him. The Lord does not see things the way you see them. People judge by outward appearance, but the Lord looks at the heart" (NLT).

Jesse paraded all seven sons of his in front of Samuel, but God rejected all of them. Finally, Samuel said, "You must have another son because God has not chosen any of these." Jesse admitted that he had one more, but he was just a young shepherd boy. Surely, God could not mean him. However, when David was brought before Samuel, he noted, "He was dark and handsome with beautiful eyes. And the Lord said, 'This is the one, anoint him!" I Samuel 16:12b (NLT). David, as we know, became a "man after God's own heart." When we trust completely in God, He will always clear up the confusion.

Personal Note:

Although confused about my future, I kept living day by day, doing what He asked of me, but still not feeling like I was contributing much in His kingdom. Nevertheless, I kept trying to obey a step at a time.

In March 2006, I started writing this devotional. He is the clarifier of my confusion. I now have direction and purpose. I know I can count on Him to complete His reasoning to bring about growth in me, before He ever takes me to the next step.

Prayer:

Father, all I need to do is simply trust You. So often, my own will gets in the way. Help me to take one step at a time and not try to outthink You. Forgive me for trying to get ahead of Your will for me. In Jesus' name, Amen.

Your Reflections:

Day 63

God is . . . Our Confidant

Bible Reading: Psalms 27:1-6

We live in an age of great uncertainty, whether it is personal, job-related, or even weather influencing. Whenever we start to go through a confusing incident in our lives, we tend to either overreact, or internalize it and hope it will go away. Neither of these approaches brings about good outcomes. We usually end up more confused and angry, blaming others or ourselves.

Hurricane Katrina is a good example of this. It was devastating for so many people, and only a day or two later we started playing the "blame game." There certainly was enough to go around, but it did not solve anything.

When we go through something devastating, it is so much better for us if we go to the Father. He already knows what we are going through, but it is very healing to confide in Him. David was an excellent example of lamenting to God. In fact, the majority of the psalms that he wrote were crying out to God to help him in his times of trouble.

"Listen to my prayer, O God. Do not ignore my cry for help! Please listen and answer me, for I am overwhelmed by my troubles" Psalm 55:1-2 (NLT). The entire psalm is about David giving over his troubles to his God. David knew who his Confidant was. God was the only One who knew David inside and out. Maybe this is one of the reasons that God called him, "a man after His own heart." David knew how to bring everything to His Maker.

Personal Note:

From my journal on July 14, 2000: "When I am faced with confusion or difficulties, it is so easy to ignore it. I do it all the time. I need to confront it, allow the feeling to manifest itself and face up to it. The more often I try to internalize my hurts the more harmful it is to my body, soul and spirit. I usually will gnaw on something and let it eat me up before I bring it to God. No! That is the wrong way! The quicker I face up to my need for help, feel it, own it, and move on, the better it is for me—body, soul and spirit."

Praise the Lord I have grown in this area. Why I think I need to carry my troubles and burdens is beyond me. Somehow, I have the mistaken idea that I am strong, or that I can solve my own problems. That is very wrong! God wants me, with a sincere heart, to bring everything before Him. He does not need fancy words and phrases but simply talking to Him. Some of my quickest solutions have been when I merely cried out to God and said, "Help me! I can't do this!" When I turn it over to Him promptly and completely, He is always there. My Confidant, my Deliverer.

Prayer:

Father, Help me to quickly turn to You and allow You to be my Confidant. I lay down my life before You and ask You to help me to bring things before You, not try to bear them on my own. Build my faith, dear Lord, in Jesus' name, Amen.

Your Reflections:

Day 64

God is . . . Forgiveness

Bible Reading: Psalm 32:1-5

Most of us know the song, "What a Friend We Have in Jesus." It is a beautiful song but much harder to live what we sing.

> *"What a friend we have in Jesus,*
> *All our sins and grief to bear.*
> *What a privilege it is to carry,*
> *Everything to God in prayer."*
> *Written by Joseph M. Scriven*

If we could leave the communication lines wide open for God's forgiveness, how much easier life would be. "And I will forgive their wickedness and I will never again remember their sins" Hebrews 8:12 (NLT). Forgiveness is so hard for us. How much joy we miss, however, because we do not bring all our sins and sorrows to God and ask His forgiveness first!

Forgiveness is something that we sometimes take lightly. It often takes blatant sin to bring us back to a repentant heart. King David was one who seldom forgot God's forgiveness. Nevertheless, when he did, he always shared with God the depth of his sin and a deep repentant heart. He was very grateful that his God, who was totally pure and blameless, could and would, fully forgive his sins.

This psalm starts out very positive. "Oh, what joy for those whose disobedience is forgiven, whose sin is put out of sight! Yes, what joy for those whose record the Lord has cleared of guilt whose lives are lived in complete honesty!" Psalm 32:1-2 (NLT). David also wrote that whenever he does not ask God for forgiveness, his body wastes away and he groans all day long! Have you ever felt that way? I have! It is much harder sometimes figuring out that I have not laid my burden at His feet; and it can be a long and painful process before I realize my error.

Personal Note:

From my journal on July 14, 2000: "It is not easy for me to get in touch with my deepest feelings, because I am so used to burying my emotions. Too many hurts have taught me to bury them as a survival mechanism. Instead of getting things solved immediately, I hide my feelings. I try to bring them to God, but only leave the door open a crack, and then I slam it shut again. This is an area where I really need His help!"

God does not want me to handle my hard times in this way. I am learning that when I bring things quickly to Him, He handles them much better than I ever could. He knows my innermost thoughts and feelings so, of course, I should go to Him. Why I do not do that immediately is still a mystery. However, I am learning to depend on Him and bring things to Him sooner and more completely.

I have a freedom in this, which has come through some "tough growing" in Him. We do not always learn our lessons quickly! One thing I can count on is that His exoneration is right there every time! Accepting His clemency is much harder! However, I cannot truly understand God's forgiveness until I can allow His mercy to wash over me and accept it. This definitely is a work in progress!

Prayer:

Thank You, Father, that no matter how long it takes to learn to agree to your forgiveness, it is always there just waiting for me to reach out and grab hold of it. You are truly a merciful God. In Jesus' name, Amen.

Your Reflections:

Day 65

God is . . . The Pillar of Cloud

Bible Reading: Exodus 33:7-11

One of my very favorite things to observe in the spring, is the clouds. They are so gorgeous with their many shapes and forms. When the sunlight beam cuts through a billowy cloud, it always reminds me of the light of Lights who shines forth from Heaven. It looks like Jesus could come any minute. Nevertheless, as many times as I have looked at the clouds, I have never seen a pillar of cloud.

Moses and the children of Israel did. It went before them daily. I cannot even imagine what it must have been like for Moses to have such a strong image of God with him constantly. One of the first things that they did whenever they came to a new camping spot was to set up the tent of meeting outside of the camp.

The people watched as Moses would make his way out to the tent of meeting. As he entered the tent, the pillar of cloud would hover at its entrance while the Lord spoke to Moses. I have tried to get a clear picture of what that "pillar of cloud" looked like. A pillar is a long round column. I try to imagine God as a pillar. It must have been an amazing sight. How could you ever forget something like that?

"Inside the tent of meeting the Lord would speak to Moses face to face as one speaks to a friend" Exodus 33:11a (NLT). However, Moses wanted even more of God. "If it is true, that You look favorably on me; let me know Your ways so I may understand you more fully and continue to enjoy your favor" Exodus 33:13 (NLT). No wonder God loved Moses so much! He could never get enough of his God.

Personal Note:

Moses was entirely open and free to accept everything about his God. As I continue on this journey with my Father, my goal is to not only leave the windows of my heart open to Him, but also open all the doors and secret places as well! I am not there yet. I am not sure any of us ever arrives there, but I am closer than I used to be. I just want more and more of my Father. How can I give more to others if I do not have more of Him? He is my Pillar of Cloud. I want Him hovering in every area of my heart. He is there! However, I do not always have the doors and windows open. How precious it is though, when I open up and have the pillar of cloud filling my heart with His presence. How my heart yearns for Him!

Prayer:

Oh, Father, Thank You for speaking to me, You always do when I am listening to You. Please hover close so that I can feel Your presence in a more intimate way. Help me to know Your ways better as I grow in You. In Jesus' name, Amen.

Your Reflections:

Day 66

God is . . . The Burden Lifter

Bible Reading: Matthew 26:36-44

Whenever we face difficult circumstances, we often carry them or "stress" over them a while. Sometimes we never give them up. On the other hand, Jesus continually knew to bring every care, worry or sorrow to God the Father, our Burden Lifter. This makes common sense. If God created us, knew us and formed us even before we were in our mother's womb, why would He not know how to solve any problem that arises in our lives?

I believe that Jesus knew that He was destined to die for our sins. However, it is not clear to me how far in advance that He knew the exact timing of those events. As the day drew near, He definitely knew His death was imminent. He often spoke to His disciples about His purpose on earth. He must die! He did not come to earth at that time to be our victorious King.

When He had the last supper with His disciples, He told them many things. I believe that He tried to explain to them the coming events, but their minds and hearts were not ready to understand what He was saying. His sorrow was so deep that night when He went into the garden of Gethsemane; He was literally carrying the weight of the whole world on His shoulders.

However, He did not keep that load to Himself He went right to prayer. What a heart-rending prayer it was! "He went on a little farther and bowed with His face to the ground, praying. My Father, if it is possible, let this cup of suffering be taken away from me. Yet, I want Your will to be done, not mine!" Matthew 26:39 (NLT). He did this three times. His resolve was complete. He clearly knew what He must do!

Personal Note:

Are we that confident in our Burden Lifter? We certainly can be. God in His infinite wisdom does not allow us to look into the future. If we knew in advance some of what we must go through, I am not sure whether we would have the courage to go through the hurt, pain and sorrow involved. That is why it is so important for me to bring every burden, every concern right to the source—My Burden Lifter!

I am learning to talk more directly to Him and tell Him about my concerns, but I still find myself carrying a heavy load at times. I know that when I do He is sad because He always wants what is best for me. He wants me to have absolute trust in Him, and an openness to allow Him to carry my burdens.

Prayer:

Thank You, Father, that You know everything about me. You are familiar with all of my ways. Nothing is too big or too small for You. You know every thought I have and You want to lighten my load. Help me to allow You to carry my burdens. In Jesus' name, Amen.

Your Reflections:

Day 67

God is . . . The Open Road

Bible Reading: 2 Kings 20:16-19

It seems like each year as our population increases we have more cars on our roadways. It is hard for our highways to accommodate the challenge for more space. Often, by the time we receive approval for more lanes or a new road, we have almost reached the need for even more roadwork to be done. Detours and delays are commonplace among us. We are very happy when we can again get back on our planned route.

Hezekiah was on the right road. He was following God's will, but hit a cul-de-sac when it came to planning for the future. He was a king of Judah. He ruled at a time when his own father, Ahaz, had closed the temple. He had boarded it up and followed his own gods. However, Hezekiah loved God Almighty and great reform happened under his rule. He reopened the temple and reestablished the Passover. He did a thorough housecleaning among the people, removing their gods and brought about their worship of the true God.

He fixed the past and made sure the present was secure, but he had little interest beyond his own reign. Because of his lack of vision for the future, his kingdom was ripe and ready for a takeover from the powerful Babylonians. Isaiah the prophet came to Hezekiah and told him that if he did not prepare better, Judah would eventually be conquered by Babylon. Hezekiah was just relieved that it would not happen under his reign.

He found out that the Assyrians had their eye on invading Judah, so he took King Sennacherib's blasphemous letter right where he should, to God Almighty. He went to the temple and laid the letter at His Maker's feet. "Now O Lord our God, rescue us from his power;

then all the kingdoms of the earth will know that you alone, O Lord, are God" 2 Kings 19:19 (NLT).

Because he had become proud, but then repented, God promised Hezekiah that he was forgiven but that the future for Judah did not look as bright. "Then Isaiah said to Hezekiah, 'Listen to this message from the Lord. The time is coming when everything in your palace—all the treasures stored up by your ancestors until now—will be carried off to Babylon. Nothing will be left,' says the Lord. 'Some of your very own sons will be taken away into exile. They will become eunuchs who will serve in the palace of Babylon's king.' Then Hezekiah said to Isaiah, 'This message you have given me from the Lord is good!' For the king was thinking, at least there will be peace and security during my lifetime" 2 Kings 20:16-19 (NLT).

I don't know about you, but to me this was not good news! Hezekiah was at best, shortsighted. He was on a big cul-de-sac! God's road is wide open, even though it is also narrow. "You can enter God's Kingdom only through the narrow gate. The highway to hell is broad and its gate is wide for the many that choose that way" Matthew 7:13 (NLT). Sometimes our thinking is mixed up and we get off the beaten path, until we start to focus back on where God's road is really leading. Even though Hezekiah got off track, God still rated him among the "good" kings. When we stray, our Father will always put us back on the open road. How merciful He is to us!

Personal Note:

On my journey, I have hit many cul-de-sacs along the way. I take my eyes off God's plan and, lo and behold, there is another dead-end! Even though God's road is wide open, it does become rocky, weatherworn and very narrow sometimes. At times, I hit a pothole and just cannot understand how this could possibly be the right road. However, our loving Father, will never take us down a road that is not His purpose for us. We may not be able to see the end, but we must still keep walking the walk and not go down those detours.

Prayer:

Father, thank You that You are a God of direction. Your way is always the straight and narrow way. Help me to keep my focus on You, so that I do not become distracted and get sidetracked. In Jesus' name, Amen.

Your Reflections:

Day 68

God is . . . The Answer to Loneliness

Bible Reading: Mark 15:33-39

Have you ever felt lonely, or rejected, even when people are around you? I have, many times. It is not a pleasant thing. Nevertheless, it pales in comparison to the loneliness that our Savior endured. He was the loneliest man who ever lived! When He was on the cross, He cried out to the Father. "And at the ninth hour, Jesus cried out in a loud voice, 'Eloi, Eloi, lama sabachthanani?' which means, "My God, my God, why have You forsaken me?" Mark 15:34 (NIV). What a heart-wrenching cry! Jesus, the Son of God, who had a myriad of angels at His beck and call, faced this awful death for the sins of all of us and He had to do it alone! He could not even call on His Father, God, because the Father's holiness could not look on sin. He had to reject His own Son, so that we could be redeemed. Christ experienced a rejection deeper than anything that we could ever feel.

I am sure that God's heart was broken as well. The moment that His Son needed His Father the most, He could not be there. He had to abandon His own Son! Oh, how great His sacrifice, how blessed we are because Christ paid that price for us! God will never reject us. We read in the Psalms "Even if my father and mother abandon me, the Lord will hold me close" Psalm 27:10 (NLT). What an awesome price He paid,—but oh, what love!

Personal Note:

Whenever we are going through hard times, loneliness, and hurts, we can be assured that we will never face anything that comes close to what Jesus had to go through on the cross. Christ bore it all for us, first. We will never face any pain, trial, or suffering that He has not borne. He went through everything that we have ever felt in our whole lives! He did so that we might have the freedom of realizing that He truly knows, loves, and cares about every detail of every moment of each day of our lives. He chose us before the foundations of the earth were laid! "How great is the love the Father has lavished on us, that we should be called children of God!" I John 3:1 (NIV).

It just does not get any better than that—lavished with love! I may yearn for that kind of love down here on earth; but because I am a human, I am limited. I cannot fully meet another's need. However, when I get, to heaven, what a time of rejoicing that will be! I can be confident that I will never again feel lonely, hurt, or suffer pain. The best part of it will be that I will be lavished with love. I will be in the very presence of my Lord! I cannot even imagine what that will be like!

Prayer:

Father, in my moment of trial when I feel so lonely, guide me in the realization that You truly know what I am facing. Help me to remember that You are always very close and that all I need to do is trust in Your love. Thank You for my Redeemer who bore all my loneliness. In His name, Amen.

Your Reflections:

Day 69

God is . . . A Confidence-Builder

Bible Reading: Psalm 27:1-6

We see repeatedly in the Bible the "great" examples of the men and women who had so much confidence in their God that they could not be shaken. Abraham stands out in this way. How many of us, if God asked us to kill our only son, would just follow God's orders and be willing to do it? Abraham had so much confidence in His God that he knew that God would provide another way. He obediently went right to the brink of stabbing Isaac; and I believe, would have done so, if God had not said, "Stop!" His confidence was in God's promise that He would make of him a great nation and that "the promise" would come through his son Isaac. Would we have forgotten all about that in the emotion of losing our son?

I think I would have questioned God and said, "God, I must have misunderstood Your directions. You can't mean that You want me to kill my son Isaac. This has to be a mistake!" However, we do not read anything like that with Abraham. He had confidence in his God, and he knew that if it meant killing Isaac, God would bring him back to life because Isaac was God's promise.

David wrote, "The Lord is my light and my salvation, so why should I be afraid? The Lord is my fortress protecting me from danger, so why should I tremble?" Psalm 27:1-2 (NLT). I believe that Abraham had that kind of confidence in His God. He knew that when God made a promise, He would fulfill it; and if man got in the way of God's plan, God would still work around it to accomplish His divine purpose.

Personal Note:

God is the same today as He has always been. If He makes a promise to us, He will keep it. So why do I not trust Him more? I believe that it is my own willfulness. I know down deep, that I certainly cannot know how to do something better than the God who made everything. Nevertheless, it is that old "control issue." I can be too human at times and want to do things my own way.

Frank Sinatra had a huge hit with his song, "I Did It My Way." I never liked that song because it left God so far out of a person's decisions. Maybe I didn't like the song because it hit too close to home. Deep inside is my self-centeredness that eats at me and urges me to want things my way. I am learning, however, to trust my God more each day.

When I listen to Him, my life goes smoothly and He works everything for my good. He builds my confidence and takes my burdens upon Himself. Who could ask for more than that?

Prayer:

Thank You, Father, that You never let me down! My life will always be on the right course when I allow You to be my confidence. Thank You for Your Son, Jesus, in whose name I pray this, Amen.

Your Reflections:

Day 70

God is . . . Silver Promises

Bible Reading: Psalm 12:5-8

How firm are your promises? I have to admit that I have promised things and meant them sincerely, but have not always fulfilled them. I think that sometimes we just speak before we really think or consider our schedules. Frequently we make commitments that are just impossible to keep. How often have we scheduled something and really thought that we could do it; then we looked at our calendars and were ashamed to find that we would need to cancel something.

In the fast-paced world that we live in, it is almost impossible to keep our commitments. Sometimes we cancel a promise to a loved one in favor of someone we do not even care about just because we know that our loved one will understand. Many times, it is a business decision that creates such chaos in our lives. Whatever the circumstance, I am sure that most of us would have to plead "guilty" at times when it comes to keeping our promise.

When I was reading this psalm, I could see how far I missed the mark of how God keeps His promises. The psalmist wrote, "The Lord's promises are pure, like silver refined in a furnace, purified seven times over!" Psalm 12:6 (NLT). Wow! What an awesome picture.

We can completely depend on our Father to fulfill His promises. He oversees the whole universe and makes sure that everything is kept in its perfect place, yet He is never too busy to keep His promises. "For Your kingdom is an everlasting kingdom, You rule throughout all generations" Psalm 145:13 (NLT). The Lord faithfully keeps His promises. He is gracious in everything He does. His calendar has room for each one individually to come before Him. He never has to "reschedule" us. He must look down on us sometimes, as a loving

Father does a child, and shake His head in wonderment at the busyness and lack of commitment we create for ourselves.

Personal Note:

People are respected for how busy they appear. For instance, we cannot go anywhere today without seeing someone talking on a cell phone. Much of the time, there is no time for a break, or lunch, or even grocery shopping. Many think that their whole lives are their careers. They step all over each other to become more successful and more important; but for too many, their lives are empty shells.

David talks about how God protects us, "Therefore, Lord, we know You will protect the oppressed, preserving them forever from this lying generation, even though the wicked strut about and evil is praised throughout the land" Psalm 12:7-8 (NLT).

I can be in the midst of this tumultuous time, but God's promises will protect and preserve me through it! I am at the stage of life when I should not have to be in the "rat race" as much. However, I still need to keep working on being true to my commitments. I know the Lord will help me, as I trust in Him more and more!

Prayer:

Father, thank You for Your promises that are as pure as refined silver that will never fail. I thank You that You can keep me calm and committed to the promises You've made though I am surrounded with stress all around me. In Jesus' name, Amen.

Your Reflections:

Day 71

God is . . . Astonishing

Bible Reading: Luke 24:13-32

Sometimes it is very hard to believe in a true miracle. Our rational minds want to come up with a levelheaded explanation. It really was no different in Jesus' day. He told His disciples and those close to Him that He was the Messiah, the Chosen One for whom they had been searching throughout all generations.

Yet when God performed the biggest miracle of all, the resurrection, everyone was utterly astonished, unbelieving, in shock and confused. Had Jesus not told them this would happen? Of course, He had! Many times and in many ways, yet the amazement was widespread throughout Judea that first Sunday after His death.

Luke describes this in the account of the two believers who were traveling on the road to Emmaus talking, going over all of the events of the past three days. Suddenly, a stranger joined them and asked them what all the fuss was? They told Him all about those past three day, how the women went to the tomb and found it empty and how Peter and John had verified it.

Jesus unfolded all of the writings of Moses and the prophets concerning His death and resurrection and still they did not recognize Him. It was not until He agreed to go home with them and they were ready to eat that it dawned on them. "As they sat down to eat, He took the bread and blessed it. Then He broke it and gave it to them. Suddenly, their eyes were opened and they recognized Him. At that moment He disappeared" Luke 24:30-31 (NLT). How astonishing! Now *that* is something to tell your grandchildren!

Personal Note:

It has always been interesting to me that the first people to find out about the resurrection, and then see Jesus in person, were women and two ordinary men. You would think that the first place Jesus would go would be to His disciples. However, He wanted to establish the astounding fact to ordinary people first.

God is still in the business of revealing His astonishing works to ordinary people today. Not that He does not use famous or special people like ministers, etc. It is just that He is the same God today as He was yesterday; and when He wants to do an amazing thing, He often uses an ordinary vessel, one that is unexpected to us, and that proves that He is a miracle-working God.

Prayer:

Thank You, Father, for Your incredible acts. They are easy for You; but as human beings, we often find them unusual and astounding. Help me to accept Your divine power in my every day living. In Jesus' name, Amen.

Your Reflections:

Day 72

God is . . . Reclusively Silent

Bible Reading: John 11:1-14

Have you ever asked God for something important only to feel complete silence on His end? I am sure that most of us have. We feel so alone, like we are talking to a wall. Mary and Martha must have felt that way.

Jesus had been a close friend of the family. He often stayed at their home when he was in their area. He loved them all and had a special bond with Lazarus, their brother. When Lazarus became very ill, they immediately sent word to Jesus. They waited patiently, but Jesus did not come. How confusing! What was going on? There was no apparent response at all! They must have felt betrayed by their friend who had healed so many others.

Had Jesus really ignored them in their hour of need? Of course not! He knew that a greater miracle was needed to fulfill the larger picture. When He arrived, Lazarus was dead. Both sisters chided Him the same way. "Lord, if You had been here, our brother would not have died!" That probably was a very accurate statement. However, neither would the Father have been glorified the way He was going to be, when Jesus raised Lazarus from the grave.

How easy it is for us to tell God, "if You had answered this prayer the way I wanted You to, everything would have been OK by now!" However, God's reclusive silence always has in mind the total picture, the total purpose and the total plan. "The Lord will work out His plans for my life—for Your faithful love, O Lord, endures forever. Don't abandon me, for You made me" Psalm 138:8 (NLT). We only have today and yesterday to look at. God has the whole future at His disposal. It may seem like He is painfully silent. Nevertheless, He is quietly working out His destiny for us.

Personal Note:

From my journal on August 20, 2000: "Unanswered prayer has always been a dilemma for me. I have never felt I could question God. However, as I am becoming more familiar with Scripture, I realize that those closest to God are never afraid to question Him and even lash out at Him in agony of soul. I need to be more comfortable with talking to Him and baring my soul. Right now, I am in a desert place where I feel that I cannot reach Him. 'Father, help me through this barren land and help me to trust You more."

I do not remember exactly what I was going through at that time, but I am now able to bring anything before my Father. David was one of our best examples of coming before God in his agony and anguish. The psalms are full of his despair but he always came back to knowing God would take care of his problems. Psalm 55:1-2 is one example: "Listen to my prayer, O God, do not ignore my plea; hear me and answer me. My thoughts trouble me and I am distraught" (NIV). God will always answer our pleas and our hurts. He knows the overall picture; and we must trust His reclusive silence.

Prayer:

Father, thank You for being very near to me no matter what the circumstances. I know that at times it may not feel like You are close, but my heart knows that You are. Help me to wait patiently on Your sovereign timing. In Jesus' name, Amen.

Your Reflections:

Day 73

God is . . . One Who Delays His Reply

Bible Reading: Habakkuk 1:1-5

We live in a generation of "instants." Whether it is coffee, oatmeal, or access to the internet, we expect something to happen immediately. Often when we pray, we want God to give us an answer instantly. God must smile sometimes at the conversations we try to have with Him, especially when we want Him to punish some injustice.

Habakkuk was a different kind of prophet. His dialogue was more between God and himself than it was communicating information from the Lord to Judah. He was a contemporary of Jeremiah and was a very godly man. He gives us a great example of how to have a conversation with God.

Like David, he knew how to tell God exactly how he was feeling. Like us, he was confused as to why God did not punish injustice. I think every generation throughout the ages finds it hard to see justice go unpunished.

In verse four we read, "Therefore the law is paralyzed and justice never prevails, the wicked hem in the righteous so that justice is perverted." Then God responds to Habakkuk in verse five, "Look at the nations and watch, and be utterly amazed. For I am going to do something in your days that you would not believe, even if you were told" (NIV).

We always want easy pat answers from God, ones we can readily understand. Nevertheless, sometimes God cannot answer our prayer, because we simply would not understand His answer. Habakkuk ended his three-chapter book with praise and honor to the God who holds everything in His power and might. "The Sovereign Lord is my strength! He makes me as surefooted as a deer, able to tread upon the heights" Habakkuk 3:19 (NLT).

Personal Note:

There are times when it takes years to receive an answer to prayer. Is it because God did not answer, or because I was not yet ready to acknowledge His answer? I might say, "Thy will be done," but the truth might be that I have not grown to the point where He can possibly answer my request.

As I learn to step out in faith, each time I become stronger and more open and trusting so that He is able to answer more of my concerns. His ways are so far above my ways that I just cannot grasp His abundance or purposes. When I am honestly ready then He is able to work freely in me and through me.

Prayer:

Father, help me to grow more each day as I learn to walk with You one step at a time. Help me to be able to receive what You have for me as I learn to communicate with You. In Jesus' name, Amen.

Your Reflections:

Day 74

God is . . . My Reality Check

Bible Reading: Matthew 20:20-24

Many times we ask God for things when we really do not have a clue as to what we are asking. When I was in junior high school, I thought that I wanted to be a missionary to India. I would pray and ask God to send me and then when the call did not come, I thought that I must have missed God's plan somewhere because even when missionaries would visit our church, I never felt called to go again. It was not until years later that I realized that this was not God's purpose for me.

Many times, it takes much preparation and God's timing to know His will. It is easy to let emotion guide us rather than God's direction and at times, He must give us a stern reality check in order to understand. The mother of James and John, who were in the inner circle of Jesus' disciples, was driven by passion, as well.

She knew that Christ loved her sons very much. She thought that the favor she was about to ask was just a normal thing for a mother to ask. However, she really had no idea about the subject she was asking. Matthew records this: "'Then the mother of Zebedee's sons came to Jesus with her sons and kneeling down, asked a favor of Him. What is it you want?' He asked. She said, 'Grant that one of these two sons of mine may sit at Your right and the other at Your left in Your kingdom.' 'You do not know what you are asking.' Jesus said to them. 'Can you drink the cup I am going to drink?'" Matthew 20:20-22a (NIV).

We may think that this was a ridiculous request, but how many of our requests are just as ridiculous in God's sight. When we remember that everything we do, or the rewards we obtain, is all in God's overall plan, we will not ask for silly things. Some of our requests cannot be granted, because they are plainly not appropriate either in content or in timing.

The psalmist wrote, "Listen to my prayer, O God. Do not ignore my cry for help! Please listen and answer me, for I am overwhelmed by my troubles" Psalm 55:1,2 (NLT). God always has His reasons for not answering us. Sometimes it is as simple as His timing! That is when we simply have to trust Him!

Personal Note:

When we first come into God's family, we arrive as newborn babies. Thinking of this, picture a very young child asking her mommy if she can stir the hot bubbly fudge that is cooking at a very high temperature. Will her mother answer this request? Probably not! The child could be badly burned. We often ask God for things that He knows will harm us.

I remember when my daughter was a little girl. I would lift her gently up onto the counter and allow her to stir the spaghetti or vegetables but it was always after I had turned the heat either low or off. I always cautioned her to be careful, so she would not be burned. One day she just reached over and touched the hot stove. Of course, she was hurt. She wanted to know what being burned felt like. Sometimes God will allow us to be burned—so we know how it feels. It is His way of giving us a reality check. He then can work His will in us.

Prayer:

Father, You alone know the complete picture. Help me to have assurance that You always hear my prayers, but sometimes it is not in my best interest to answer them in the way I want. Thank You that You are always my reality check. In Jesus' name, Amen.

Your Reflections:

Day 75

God is . . . Hallowed

Bible Reading: Leviticus 22:31-33

What does it mean that God is holy? For me hallowed seems a good description of His holiness. It is everything pure and righteous, which calls for a respectful and humble response. It is something that we as humans cannot achieve on our own. I read a survey recently in which people were asked if they were holy. Twenty-one percent of them said, "Yes!" Seventy-three percent said that they could become holy in spite of their past. That is astounding to me! It just proved that we do not know the first thing in relation to what being holy is about.

To quote our reading for today, "Therefore you shall keep my commandments, and perform them: I am the Lord. You shall not profane My holy name, but I will be hallowed among the children of Israel. I am the Lord who sanctifies you, who brought you out of the land of Egypt, to be your God. *I am* the Lord" Leviticus 22:31-33 (NKJ).

When God set the rules for Moses and the people of Israel, many of them were to produce and protect purity and holiness in the people. God knew none of us is without sin so He had the priest bring a sacrifice of an animal to represent our sin.

The priest went through a very extensive purifying process. Only after this extreme act and a meticulous rule of offering a perfect lamb as the substitute for the people's sin, could the priest present the sacrifice up to God and the sins be made pure enough to be forgiven.

God alone can make something holy. Remember when God spoke to Moses through the burning bush, He said, "take off your sandals, for the place you are standing is holy ground" Exodus 3:5b (NIV). Anytime that God came to man, His holiness was so pure, that even the most righteous were limited in how close they could come to Him.

Jesus, when He was teaching us how to pray, said, "Our Father in heaven, hallowed be Thy name" Matthew 6:9 (NIV). Holiness is the very nature of God and must not be taken lightly.

Personal Note:

I believe that after Jesus' resurrection, when He told Mary Magdalene not to touch Him because he had not yet gone to the Father, this was all a part of the "new covenant in His blood." He had His new body. His body had been hallowed. He did give His disciples' permission to place their fingers in His hands and side, but I believe that was to show our new access to Him. Now all of us might enter and come to God's holiness, with the purity and sanctity that God requires because He sees us only through His Son's perfection.

Prayer:

Our Father, hallowed be thy name! I praise You that I can come before You, through Your Son, and I can be found holy in Your sight. Because of His purity, I am made pure. What a wonderful gift You gave to me in Jesus! In Your holy name, Amen.

Your Reflections:

Day 76

God is . . . The Ultimate Perspective

Bible Reading: Jonah 1:1-12

One of the things I love about the Bible is that it shows the flaws of our humanity as well as the lessons we need to learn. The book of Jonah is a good example. We read this familiar story and remember Jonah being swallowed by the fish; but do we remember why this all came about in the first place? The book of Jonah begins by revealing the problem.

Jonah was a prophet of the Lord. He was from Israel and lived at the time when Jeroboam II was king in Israel, sometime between 793-753 BC. Their most dreaded enemy was Assyria and its capitol was Nineveh.

When God told Jonah that He wanted him to go and preach repentance to Nineveh, Jonah did not want any part of it! He boarded the first ship he could find that was going in the opposite direction. There was no way that he was going to go to his enemy and tell them to repent and turn to God. It was not until he was thrown overboard and swallowed by a fish, that Jonah started to give up his rebellious ways. Even then, he was in the belly of the fish for three days. I cannot even imagine how disgusting that must have been!

He finally did go to Nineveh, and the people repented, which still made Jonah upset. In fact, he was downright angry with God because God had mercy on the people and withheld His hand of judgment on them. Jonah went outside the city and sat down to sulk.

"Didn't I say before I left home that You would do this, Lord? That is why I ran away to Tarshish! I knew that You are a merciful and compassionate God, slow to get angry and filled with unfailing love.

You are eager to turn back from destroying people. Just kill me now, Lord! I'd rather be dead than alive if what I predicted will not happen" Jonah 4:2b-3 (NLT). Jonah was one unhappy prophet. Nevertheless, in the end, God's plan prevailed—and it always will.

Personal Note:

There are many great lessons to be learned from Jonah. Preparation is one of them. When I pray, I need to know that I am really prepared for His answer. Sometimes God will answer my prayer, and I may not like His answer at all. I may even request something that I know is the right thing, but His answer can be very different from what I thought I was asking. For example, "Lord, bring me closer to you!" I have prayed that often; but many times the process of trial and testing that I must go through to get there is very painful and much harder than what I bargained for.

Another lesson that Jonah teaches me is that I need to have confidence that God will always do what completes His purpose. I must go through some very hard places at times and I may not like His plan, but His ways are perfect. I can kick and scream all I want but ultimately, His mission will be accomplished. Just like Jonah, God will prove His sovereignty over and above my selfish perspective. His omnipotence is unquestionable and above understanding. That is when trust must take over. What a lesson! However, if I learn it, what blessing awaits me.

Prayer:

Father, thank You for responding to my needs even when I do not understand Your answer. Help me to learn to rely completely on You as You bring Your purpose to fulfillment through me. In Jesus' name, Amen.

Your Reflections:

Day 77

God is . . . The Perfect Number

Bible Reading: Genesis 7:1-5

Biblical numbers have always fascinated me. It is amazing that God gave me this thought for today, Day 77. After all, it is His perfect number! He gave us seven days of the week. He also created the world in seven days. As I read scripture, I find many places where the Lord has used His perfect number. When He instructed Noah, He told him "Take with you seven of every kind of clean animal, a male and its mate, and two of every kind of unclean animal, a male and its mate, and also seven of every kind of bird, male and female, to keep their various kinds alive throughout the earth" Genesis 7:2-3 (NIV).

Other numbers have real significance to God. Pastor Adrian Rogers, in one of his sermons, related some numbers that are symbolic of God's order. These are some of them:

One is for God
Two is a witness. Like two or more agreeing on something or two of a kind like male and female.
Three symbolizes the Trinity, or His Divine nature.
Four refers to all of nature, creation or earth.
Five is the number of completeness, or fullness.
Six is man's number.
Seven is God's Perfect Number or the number of completion.
Eight represents a new start, or beginnings.
Twelve stands for God's ruling or governing factors. (i.e.; twelve tribes of Israel, twelve Apostles who will sit on twelve thrones in heaven, etc.

These numbers represent just a few of the many ways that God shows us His organization and order through His Word. How detailed our Father is! What a wonderful guideline He has given us. We use numbers today as a form of order in our lives as well. The psalmist wrote, "So teach us to number our days, that we may gain a heart of wisdom" Psalm 90:12 (NKJ). He is the ultimate teacher, and with his wisdom, we can turn chaos and confusion into order and structure.

Personal Note:

I wonder, at times, if my fascination with numbers goes back to when I was a little girl. I used to lie on my front lawn in the warm summer evenings and try to count the stars. Of course, I never came anywhere close to doing so; but at that time, bright city lights or pollution did not dim the stars and the sky was so very beautiful. It makes me think of how God showed Abraham the stars of the sky and told him that His descendents would number as many as the stars in the heavens.

How personal our Father is! He shows me, as well, how very much He loves me by reminding me of how important counting and numbers are to Him. One of my favorite examples is "And even the very hairs of your head are all numbered" Matthew 10:30 (NIV). Oh, how I love this second one: "You keep track of all my sorrows, You have collected all my tears in Your bottle. You have recorded each one in Your book" Psalm 56:8 (NLT). Yes, my God loves order. He prepared me to live at exactly this time in history and has every day of my life carefully counted. How awesome! How perfect!

Prayer:

Father, thank You for creating everything in this universe in an orderly manner. You have a purpose in everything. You are truly perfect and methodical in all Your ways. Help me to learn to be more organized in my life as You have shown me so clearly in Your Word. Thank you, in Jesus' name, Amen.

Your Reflections:

Day 78

God is . . . Our Soul-Searcher

Bible Reading: James 4:7-10

Whenever I really desire to come close to God, the Holy Spirit begins a soul-searching that shows me the areas of my heart that need refining. It's like having God turn on this huge light and check every corner of my heart. This can be a very painful process as God reveals areas of my soul that I find difficult to give up. I become vulnerable to feelings that I may have had buried deep inside.

Spiritual growth is a process. For many of us it takes numerous years for God to work out His plan in our lives. James gives us a wonderful pattern to live by. "So humble yourselves before God. Resist the devil and he will flee from you. Come close to God and God will come close to you" James 4:7 (NLT).

These are wonderful instructions from James. They sound so easy, but many times, it is a hard struggle. I hold on to control as if it is my most cherished possession. Oh how I love to be in my comfort zone. However, I seem to hold on to the hurts in life as well. I wallow in self-pity and tend to nurse the pain, rather than giving it over to God.

An issue for many of us is judging or criticizing one another, even when we think we are not judgmental or critical. If we take a good look at ourselves through God's eyes, more than likely we have areas of our hearts that are biased toward others. We tend to appraise them by our own personal standards.

God is different. He is the only One who can judge with absolute fairness. Matthew wrote, "Do not judge others and you will not be judged. For you will be treated as you treat others. The standard you use in judging is the standard by which you will be judged" Matthew

7:1,2 (NLT). Do I really want God to use His standard of measure on me? If I judge by God's standard, I will be busy fixing my own weaknesses and will not have time to criticize another. For me that is a goal worth achieving!

Personal Note:

I know that as God is searching my own life I fall far short of what I want to be in Him. Nevertheless, it is interesting that the closer I come to God the less I criticize others. When I genuinely want Him to search me, cleanse me and make me into His image, He does so! I have never known Him to fail me. His love surpasses my pettiness so significantly that He instantly forgives me and remembers my weakness no more! Many times, I have a much greater problem accepting His forgiveness than He ever does forgiving me. What a blessing, however, when I can fully forgive as He forgives me.

Prayer:

Father, I pray that You will continue Your soul-searching in my life. Help me to look inward and not outward at others. I pray that as I search my own heart that I will be able to accept Your forgiveness, as You forgive me. In Christ's name, Amen.

Your Reflections:

Day 79

God is . . . Knowledge

Bible Reading: 2 Peter 1:3-10

We live in an age where knowledge abounds at a pace that we have never experienced before. The technical revolution ushered in an era of information and understanding that has soared in the last ten years. However, with all of our technical understanding, we have lost the most important information of all—that Christ came to give us life more abundantly and fill us with the wisdom of God.

Peter lived in a culture where the quest for knowledge was at a peak. He wanted to make sure that Christians of his day had the right instruction to help them along the right path. He wrote his letter two or three years after Nero started persecuting the Christians. You can feel the intensity and urgency in Peter's message. He is speaking mainly to Jewish Christians to whom He has been ministering. He informs them that the times they are living in are extremely dangerous.

In fact, he knows that his own time is short here on earth and he shares this with them: "For our Lord Jesus Christ has shown me that I must soon leave this earthly life" 2 Peter 1:14 (NLT). It was not long before he would be dying on a cross like His Lord. He felt that he was unworthy to die like Christ, so he requested to be hung on the cross upside down. What spiritual growth Peter had since the day that he denied ever knowing His Lord and Master.

He concludes His writing by stating, "I am warning you ahead of time, dear friends, be on guard so that you will not be carried away by the errors of these wicked people and lose your own secure footing. Rather, you must grow in the grace and knowledge of our Lord and Savior Jesus Christ. All glory to Him, both now and forever! Amen" 2 Peter 3:17,18 (NLT).

Personal Note:

*God's knowledge is how I grow as well. He has given me His Word, the Bible; and His **Word**, Jesus Christ. The more I read the Bible, the more I will grow in the knowledge that God has for me, both in His Word and in His Son. The Bible is His way of directing me in my life. Once I started to read it on a regular basis, God spoke to me through its pages. As I continue to read and study His Word, the Holy Bible, He will bless me, strengthen me, and edify me, as I walk in obedience to studying His Word. His enlightenment is the most important knowledge that I can acquire. No matter what accomplishments I may have in other subjects, the only source that directs my future as well as my present is His Holy Word. What a fabulous gift. What a fabulous God!*

Prayer:

Father, I thank you that You have been so generous with Your knowledge. You have revealed so much of Yourself to me. Thank You for the many blessings that You have given me, through Your Word, and through Jesus Christ, The Living Word. In His name, Amen.

Your Reflections:

Day 80

God is . . . Breathtaking

Bible Reading: Daniel 10:4-11, 15-18

One thing we find very consistently in Scripture is that when God brings mere humans into His presence, it is so astonishing that they cannot look upon Him and are unable to stand. They usually lie humbled at His feet. This is exactly how Daniel felt when God sent His messenger from heaven.

This took place after Daniel had His awesome test from God. Daniel's obedience to his God, not to bow down to the king's image, had brought him big trouble. Even though he thought that he would be martyred by being thrown to the lions, he resolved to obey God, not man. We know the story. After they threw him into the lions den, (hungry lions at that), God shut the mouths of the lions and Daniel survived without a scratch!

This extreme testing allowed God to use Daniel in a unique way. He allowed him to see into the end-times and write down what he saw. It was during these visions that God sent His messenger personally to Daniel. He describes his vision this way, "I looked up and saw a man dressed in linen clothing, with a belt of pure gold around his waist. His body looked like a precious gem. His face flashed like lightning, and his eyes flamed like torches. His arms and feet shone like polished bronze, and his voice roared like a vast multitude of people" Daniel 10:5, 6 (NLT).

After seeing such a stunning person, Daniel was very weak. He wrote, "How can someone like me, your servant, talk to You, my Lord? My strength is gone, and I can hardly breathe. Then the One who looked like a man touched me again, and I felt my strength returning. Do not be afraid, he said, for you are very precious to God. Peace!

Be encouraged! Be strong!" Daniel 10:17-19 (NLT). This amazing experience took Daniel's breath away. My finite mind cannot even imagine what an awesome experience that must have been. How breathtakingly powerful our God is!

Personal Note:

Daniel's awesome experience did not happen until after he had been in the lion's den. Often, our most incredible experiences with God are only after we go through a lion's den test.

Testing is one way that I grow. If I step out in obedience and pass the test, then God can trust me with astounding miracles and experiences. Compared to what Daniel experienced, I know that my encounters have been very small but at times, when I am in intimate prayer with my Father, He has taken my breath away with His beauty and His awesome presence. I yearn for experiences that are even more breathtaking with Him!

Prayer:

Father, when I think of You and Your love for me, You take my breath away. You are so astonishingly wonderful that I can only get a glimpse of Your presence. Thank You so much for the privilege of having a personal intimacy with You. In Jesus' name, Amen.

Your Reflections:

Day 81

God is . . . The Mighty "I AM"

Bible Reading: Exodus 3:9-15

Moses felt completely inadequate when he encountered the presence of God in the burning bush. After all, he had fled from Egypt after killing an Egyptian and had put his former life totally behind him. Now he was a humble tender of sheep, and God was asking him to go back to Egypt and rescue the Israelites. He used every excuse he could to tell God that he was not qualified to do this. He was not a good speaker and he clearly did not think the people would believe that God had sent him, so he questioned God. He said, "What would I tell them? Who would I say sent me?"

The answer came in verses 14 and 15 "God replied to Moses, 'I AM WHO I AM! Say this to the people of Israel: I AM has sent me to you!'" God also said to Moses, "'Say this to the people of Israel: Yahweh, the God of your ancestors—the God of Abraham, the God of Isaac and the God of Jacob—has sent me to you. This is my eternal name; my name is remembered for all generations'" (NLT).

I AM is the name that strengthens our weakness. It is the very essence of God. He always was, always is and always will be the same—never-changing God Almighty! The attributes of God—holiness, justice and righteousness—are all wrapped up in I AM; but the centrality of God, the motivation and essence of His character, is His all-encompassing love, perfect and unconditional! This strengthening love motivates everything else He is!

From that day forward, Moses had the powerful I AM beside him and in him. I AM, the compelling, enduring, perfect love! In Exodus 6:6 (NLT) God reaffirms His promise. "Therefore, say to the people of Israel, I AM the Lord. I will free you from your oppression and will rescue you from your slavery in Egypt. I will redeem you with a powerful arm and great acts of judgment." I AM! Yahweh! The Eternal God! Our Deliverer! How incredible!

Personal Note:

Whenever I read this passage of Scripture in the past, the name I AM was always confusing to me. I just did not understand the depth of meaning that this name included. It is hard to understand such a perfect and complete God who is self-existent when we are so finite and imperfect. For me it has taken a real process to understand that God has created me unique. Unlike any other human being.

There is only one me, and God wants to shape me into the best "me" I can be. He is the only one who can do that. Nevertheless, in order for Him to use me, I have to give Him permission to open every area of my life. I have to believe that He is the all-encompassing I AM—complete in every way and in everything!

I am so grateful that He loves me that much. He loves us all, individually that much. No matter what I have done, not done, been, or not been, the fabulous I AM loves me unconditionally! I cannot do anything that would prevent Him from loving me. This is an astounding thought for me! As I grow in His love, it becomes more amazing every day.

Prayer:

My Father, how I thank You, that You are the essence of love. You are the great I AM, all encompassing. When You are in control of my life, there is absolutely nothing that is excluded. I praise Your holy name that You are everything I could ever want or need. In Jesus' name, Amen.

Your Reflections:

Day 82

God is . . . Firm Steps

Bible Reading: Psalm 121:1-8

When I was young, I wore the highest-heeled shoes that I could find. This would throw my body way off balance; and I remember taking more than one fall as I tried to maneuver cracked sidewalks and bumpy roads. This reminds me of the uncertain ground that I have walked on as I walk with my Lord.

Where do we go when our life is a bit shaky, when our steps are unsteady? God makes it plain that if we trust Him, we will never have to worry about where to go. He is like firm steps. He keeps us from going down that slippery slope of temptation. No matter what we are facing, He will be there to under gird us with His steadiness and support. We can have confidence that He will keep our steps firm. The Psalmist wrote, "I lift up my eyes to the hills—where does my help come from? My help comes from the Lord, the Maker of heaven and earth. He will not let your foot slip—He who watches over you will not slumber" Psalms 121:1-3 (NIV).

What a wonderful promise this is for us. There is another psalm that I love that David wrote about his assurance in allowing God to guide his steps. It says, "My steps have held to Your path; my feet have not slipped" Psalm 17:5 (NIV). What a wonderful statement! David knew exactly who directed His steps and there was no way that he was going to take any path other than one God had provided. There is a verse in Proverbs that says, "In his heart a man plans his course, but the Lord determines his steps" Proverbs 16:9 (NIV). I want to keep my heart on the right course in the Lord, so that He may keep my steps firmly planted in Him!

Personal Note:

From my Journal on September 16, 2000: Knowing God, His nature and His character is one of the most beneficial things I can do to strengthen my walk with Him. The more I know of Him, the deeper my walk will be and the firmer my steps. My desire is to know Him better so that I will never be shaken and my steps will remain firmly set on Him.

As I read this writing and looked back on these last several years, I am amazed at how directly He has answered that simple desire. My aspiration to know Him has deepened into a steadying force and confident knowledge that He is forever with me, guiding me, helping me walk in His firm steps, and blessing me beyond anything I could ever have imagined. My heart's craving is to continue to get to know Him in a deeper and deeper way so that my steps will be a walking testimony of His grace and mercy. I want to be His "star pupil" firmly imitating His steps!

Prayer:

Father, thank you for guiding me and allowing me to walk in Your firm steps. Help me not to falter along the way, but to put my confidence fully in You. In Jesus' name, Amen.

Your Reflections:

Day 83

God is . . . Our Fixed Point

Bible Reading: Hebrews 13:5-9

What is a "fixed point?" It is something immovable that you can focus on to find your direction. The term is commonly used in navigating ships. When heading toward the shore, the captain of a ship will find some stable object to focus on so that he can steer his ship safely to the mooring. If there is a lighthouse, then of course, that makes his navigation easier, but if not, he will focus on whatever object he can find that is unchangeable and unmovable.

Whether we are driving a car or taking a walk, we will find a point of reference and head toward it. There is built-in radar within us that needs a stable object to steer our lives. When we do not have one, we are disoriented—much like a ship would be without its fixed point. In Psalm 107:29-30 we read, "He calms the storm so that its waves are still. Then they are glad because they are quiet; so He guides them to their desired haven" (NKJ) When we turn our lives over to our God, He becomes our steadying force, our fixed point. Nothing can get us off course if we put our faith in Him.

Our Father is always watching over us just as loving parents guard their children. We watch over them so that we can keep them from getting into trouble. If we do that for our children, how much more does our Heavenly Father take care of us? He is always the same. He never changes. In the New Testament, Paul wrote, "For God has said, I will never fail you, I will never abandon you. So we can say with confidence, The Lord is my helper, so I will have no fear. What can mere people do to me?" Hebrews 13:5b-6 (NLT). He is our stability, our (immoveable) fixed point. He is always waiting for us to focus in and let Him be our security.

Personal Note:

Whenever I keep focused on my Father, no stress is too big or burden too heavy. However, if I take my thoughts away from Him and focus my attention on other things, then the cares and stresses of my fast-paced living take over and I lose my fixed point. The beautiful thing is, though, that my fixed point never moves so I can always find my way back to it again.

The chorus of a song, popular during the earlier part of my life says,

> *"Turn your eyes upon Jesus.*
> *Look full in His wonderful face.*
> *And the things of earth will grow strangely dim,*
> *In the light of His glory and grace."*
> *Words by: Helen Lemmel*

What a blessing it is to know that we have such an (unshakeable) fixed point.

Prayer:

My Father, how grateful I am that You are (unchangeable.) I can always turn to You for the right direction if I get off course. How I love You and praise You for Your stability. You are a faithful fixed point. How I thank you, in my Savior's dear name, Amen.

Your Reflections:

Day 84

God is . . . A Strong Right Arm

Bible Reading: Psalm 118:15-21

One thing that has blessed me, as I have delved deeper in the Word, is that so many Scriptures use parts of the body to give us clear images of God, such as His eyes, ears, mouth, lips, hands, fingers, legs, feet and heart. For example, in today's reading, it talks about His strong right arm. "Songs of joy and victory are sung in the camp of the godly. The strong right arm of the Lord has done glorious things. The strong right arm of the Lord is raised in triumph. The strong right arm of the Lord has done glorious things" Psalm 118:15,16 (NLT).

When we think of His strong arms, many images come to mind. As our Father, I can picture Him picking up a hungry, crying child in His mighty right arm and cradling her close to His heart. He loves little children and watches over them all. He helps us when we are going through our hard places. He covers us with His gentle protection and love.

Yet this same God with His mighty arm can calm the seas; make the rain to fall, and the sun to shine. He tells the moon when to rise and the stars to fill our skies. "He changes rivers into deserts, and springs of water into dry, thirsty land . . . But He also turns deserts into pools of water, the dry land into springs of water" Psalm 107:33,35 (NLT). With His strong right arm He rules and reigns over all. Yes, the strong right arm of the Lord has truly done glorious things!

Personal Note:

I have felt those mighty arms around me many times: when my two sisters were killed in an auto accident, when I had my miscarriages, when I heard the word "cancer" for the first time. There have been many other times as well, when I have gone through deep waters both emotionally and physically throughout my life.

How closely my Father wants to hold me. To swoop right down and pick me up in His powerful right arm and hold me to His heart. He cares so much about me! He is there even when my heart is not listening but holding back. He waits patiently for me to ask Him to encompass me in His strong right arm, to hold me closely and bring victory and healing to my brokenness. He knows everything about me—my strengths and my weaknesses, my joys and sorrows, easy times and all the hard times I am going through.

His love is so deep and strong for each one of us individually, that we can only accept a small part of it. But oh, the joy it will be when we get to heaven and can fully experience the depth of His love for us. We will understand it all then. Our Father's right arm is always reaching out to each of us. I want to reach out my arms to Him and let Him bring me closer to Him? That is my heart's desire!

Prayer:

Father, I thank You that Your strong right arm has truly done glorious things. You are my victor when I feel defeated. Your love for me is so rich and pure. I praise You for Your mighty works. In Jesus' name, Amen.

Your Reflections:

Day 85

God is . . . Our Home

Bible Reading: Psalm 90:1-5

As I grow older it does not matter whether I am gone for just an afternoon or whether I have been on a trip, I can hardly wait to get home. Home is my comfort zone; it is where I relax, where I abide. I did not really think about God being my home. I know I did subconsciously, but I am not sure that I thought of it in just this way before.

God is Eternal. He is self-existing! It is sometimes hard for us to grasp this fact. It is easy to see why, because we have no frame of reference. We were born, we live so many years and then we die. Life is a cycle. However, God does not live in a cycle. He has always been and always will be.

Our finite minds cannot even begin to comprehend this truth. Psalm 90:1-2 begins with this fact, "Lord, through all the generations You have been our home. Before the mountains were born, before You gave birth to the earth and the world, from beginning to end, You are God" (NLT). He has been "our home" through all the ages. Since He has always been here, we have Someone who we can come home to. We can never stray too far, or retreat too deeply, from everlasting to everlasting; He is always, our home. There is no place like our home! It is the place that we can kick off our shoes and get comfortable. There is no facade, just God, our home!

The Psalmist also begins the next psalm by saying, "He who dwells in the shelter of the Most High will rest in the shadow of the Almighty. I will say of the Lord, He is my refuge and my fortress, my God, in whom I trust" Psalm 91:1-2 (NIV). God wants to be our place of safety and comfort, a place that we can hardly wait to come home to! That is where I want to be, resting in my God—my home!

Personal Note:

When I was eight years old, my earthly father left us. It was just my mother, one sister and me, from that moment on. Maybe that is why I have been on this quest to know my heavenly Father more intimately. To know that He is always with me no matter what and that He will never leave me or forsake me is so incredible.

Even more amazing is the fact that He wants to pour down His riches and favor on me. All I have to do in return is to let Him have total and complete control of my life. That does not mean that I will never face difficult times here on earth. I will, and I have. Nevertheless, this Father, who has existed before anything was created, is my comfort, my home! Nothing or no one can or will ever be able to change that. What security there is in knowing that I am home when I am resting in my Father's love!

Prayer:

Father, Thank You for giving me such a wonderful, secure place. You are my home, my dwelling place, my resting place. I know that I never need to fear that You will leave me, because You have always been, and always will be with me. Forever and ever. How I praise You and love You. In Jesus' name, Amen.

Your Reflections:

Day 86

God is . . . Honorable

Bible Reading: Hebrews 8:7-13

When God makes a covenant with His people, we can be confident that He will keep it. He has proven repeatedly how honorable He is. The first covenant that He made was with Noah. After the flood, God promised that He would never destroy the entire earth by flood again. He gave us all a sign that has endured through all generations. That is the beautiful rainbow. God said that every time we look at a rainbow, we would know that God is keeping His covenant with us.

God's faithfulness is seen throughout all of the history of mankind. He made a covenant with Abraham, Moses and then David. Finally He sent His one and only Son and with Him, God gave us a new covenant. This one includes anyone and everyone who believes in His Son. Paul wrote in Hebrews, "If the first covenant had been faultless, there would have been no need for a second covenant to replace it. However, when God found fault with the people he said, 'The day is coming,' says the Lord, 'when I will make a new covenant with the people of Israel and Judah'" Hebrews 8:7,8 (NLT).

Does that mean that God broke His first covenant? Not at all! The people broke it. They became too wicked to be able to keep it any longer. God had to send His perfect Son to become the perfect sacrifice for our sins. All who accept this gift are included. It is individual, by faith. That encompasses all nations without exception.

All who believe are under the new covenant, which we commemorate every time we take communion. God will never break His new covenant because it is made perfect, through Jesus Christ. Paul recorded this, "They gave thanks to God for it. Then He broke it (the bread) in pieces and said; This is My body, which is given for you. Do this to remember me. In the same way, He took the cup of wine after supper saying; This cup is the new covenant between God and His people—an agreement confirmed with My blood. Do this to remember Me as often as You drink it" I Corinthians 11:24,25 (NLT) (*parenthesis mine*). God will never go back on His word.

Personal Note:

I am so thankful that I have a Father who, I know beyond any doubt, will always keep His word. He is the only One who is honorable. There will never be a human being I can count on completely, who will not let me down. We are all, imperfect. Because of that, we, sometimes, fail and hurt each other. When that happens, we know that we can come to our honorable Father and know that He is reliable. What a comfort that is to my soul!

Prayer:

Father, Thank You for including me in Your new covenant. I can be confident that You will always honor Your word. Thank You, Jesus, for being willing to be my perfect sacrifice so that any one who comes to You can be a part of this new covenant. In Your precious name, Amen.

Your Reflections:

Day 87

God is . . . Relenting

Bible Reading: Joel 2:11-14

One fact is true: God wants to bless us. He delights in doing good things for us. However, He will also bring judgment upon us, if we turn our backs on Him. We have seen this repeatedly throughout the history of Israel. God would send prophet after prophet to try to get the people to repent, and when they finally reached the point of no return, God would have to send His judgment.

At this period in history, God had sent a swarm of locusts to eat up all of the land of Judah, and Joel had urged the people to turn from their sin and to turn back to God. He pleaded with God that it would not be too late. Joel wrote, "The Lord says, 'turn to me now, while there is time. Give me your hearts. Come with fasting, weeping and mourning. Don't tear your clothing in your grief, but tear your hearts instead'" Joel 2:12b-13 (NLT).

Because He is a holy and righteous God, when a nation rebels against Him, many times, it takes fasting, weeping, and truly mourning our sin before He will reverse His judgment on a nation. God will always relent from His judgment when His people honestly have a repentant heart. He will then restore His people and make their nation whole again. "Bring your confessions and return to the Lord. Say to Him, Forgive all our sins and graciously receive us, so that we may offer You our praises" Hosea 14:2 (NLT).

Personal Note:

Life is a journey and my spiritual life is no different. I cannot tell you how many times I have come before my Father, humbly, and asked for His forgiveness. It seems to me that the more I grow in Him, the more I realize how very far I still need to go. The beauty of it is, though, His love surpasses His judgment. Love is the very essence of who God is. His love is so deep for us and He cares so much that He specializes in putting broken pieces back together again.

We sang a hymn that I dearly loved when I was growing up and the words have stayed with me:

> *"Have Thine own way, Lord, have Thine own way.*
> *Thou art the Potter I am the clay.*
> *Mold me and make me after Thy will.*
> *While I am waiting yielded and still."*
>   *Words by Adelaide A. Pollard*

No matter how many times I fail Him, no matter how many times I lie broken at His feet, when I come before Him humbly, He will always relent and be there to renew me again. His mercy is truly amazing!

Prayer:

Father, how I thank You that You are a relenting God. You take great joy in anyone who comes to You with a repentant heart. Restore me again, as I walk humbly before You and truly seek Your forgiveness, In Jesus' name, Amen.

Your Reflections:

Day 88

God is . . . The One for Whom I Wait

Bible Reading: Genesis 15:1-6

For most of us, waiting for God to answer our prayer is one of the more difficult things He asks us to do. We want things to happen in our time. God's timing is much different from ours.

One of the best examples of waiting, or not, is Abram. God made a promise to him when he was already too old to have children, that He would provide him with a son who would become his heir. Sarai became impatient and implied that God was not keeping His promise to them. At least ten years had passed, so she told Abram that she would give her servant Hagar to Abram to produce an heir. Abram agreed. however, when Hagar became pregnant and provided Abram with a son, there was no rejoicing over this son. There was only turmoil and heartache.

Because Abram had gone ahead of God's plan and accepted His second best rather than His ultimate purpose, God waited another decade before Abram would be ready to commit to God's total plan. He appeared to Abram and reaffirmed His covenant to include fathering many nations." God changed His name to Abraham, which means a father of many nations. God was very specific that Sarai would no longer keep her name either.

"Regarding Sarai, your wife—her name will no longer be Sarai. From now on, her name will be Sarah. I will bless her and give you a son from her! Yes, I will bless her richly, and she will become the mother of many nations" Genesis 17:15,16a (NLT). Abraham was 100 years old when Sarah gave birth to their son Isaac. God will always fulfill His promises to us, but sometimes we have to wait for His timing!

Personal Note:

How often has God had a perfect plan for me and I went ahead of Him and accepted His second best? I am sure more than I could ever imagine. There have been times in my life when I have been so impatient, stubborn and willful. I wanted to do God's will as long as it did not interfere with my way. One thing I am learning, however, is that when I completely turn my life over to Him, He has a wonderful outcome for me.

I may believe that I know how to maneuver hard places in my life, but I usually make a mess of things. The hardest thing is to realize that even if my plan goes smoothly, God may have had something even better for me if I had waited on Him. Frequently it takes a lot of pruning before I am ready to accept the responsibility of what God really wants to do within me. It is taking a lifetime to learn, and it probably will for most of us. We will never be complete and perfect until we get to heaven but for now, I want Him to keep shaping my life and teaching me what His perfect plan is for me so I will endeavor to keep waiting patiently!

Prayer:

Father, help me to be more open to Your plan and purpose in my life. Keep me from getting ahead of Your best for me. "Mold me and make me, after Your will, while I am waiting, yielded and still!" In Jesus' name, Amen.

Your Reflections:

Day 89

God is . . . Patient

Bible Reading: James 1:2-8

Patience, do I really want to talk about this? It is an area in my life where growth is needed. How difficult it is for me to wait on the Lord! However, that is exactly what brings real maturity and strength into my life. Isaiah 40:31 is a familiar passage for many of us. "But those who wait on the Lord shall renew their strength; they shall mount up with wings like eagles, they shall run and not be weary, they shall walk and not faint." (NKJ). What an awesome promise!

God is extremely patient. We see His marvelous example all through the Scripture. Paul instructs us in Romans, "Now may the God of patience and comfort grant you to be like-minded toward one another, according to Christ Jesus" Romans 15:5 (NKJ).

The Father is not alone in His patience. Paul writes, "Now may the Lord direct your hearts into the love of God and into the patience of Christ" 2 Thessalonians 3:5 (NKJ).

We also learn about the Holy Spirit. "But the Holy Spirit produces this kind of fruit in our lives: love, joy, peace, *patience,* kindness, goodness, faithfulness, gentleness and self-control. There is no law against these things" Galatians 5:22 (NLT) (*italics mine*).

The complete Godhead—Father, Son and Holy Spirit—manifest this great quality. Is it any wonder that James begins with teaching us about patience? "But let patience have its perfect work, that you may be perfect and complete, lacking nothing" James 1:4 (NKJ).

Personal Note:

We live in a society that measures our whole lives in microseconds. With the computer and technology age upon us, a second can seem like such a long time. Standing next to a microwave oven waiting for something to heat up may only take a minute, but it seems like a very long minute! Even waiting for our computers to "boot up" is an endurance challenge at times.

In the light of our fast-paced living, isn't it wonderful to realize that God, Jesus and the Holy Spirit are all there, patiently waiting, to help us learn this marvelous gift of endurance? In my case, I am more patient than I used to be, but the work certainly is not finished. What an incredible truth, though, that as I learn to practice patience, it makes me complete, lacking nothing! What a worthy goal this is!

Prayer:

Father, thank you for Your patience with me. I cannot even imagine my life if You were as impatient with me as I have been with others at times. Teach me to become more like You. In Jesus' name, Amen.

Your Reflections:

Day 90

God is . . . Nourishing the Aged Fruit

Bible Reading: Psalm 92:12-15

As I grow older, I appreciate spending more time with my heavenly Father. That is one of the blessings of aging; I have more time to pray and read His Word. It is a tremendous blessing to me to have something rich and vital to do at this stage in my life.

When we started this year's small group at church, we went around the tables introducing ourselves. We were asked to share what we enjoyed in our lives. One of the older women, Vivian, introduced herself as a widow who enjoyed visiting people. She also prays for others when she awakens in the night. That is a heart, which is ripe and aged to perfection in God's kingdom. How important she is to Him! God has a special place in His heart for widows. He asks us to take special care of them.

Throughout the Bible, we see examples of God's tender loving care for widows. One of my favorites is the story of Naomi and her daughter-in-law, Ruth. They were both widows who traveled by themselves through the dangerous desert back to Israel, so that Naomi could return to her people. She was depressed and downtrodden. She saw little hope for either of their futures to marry and have children. Everything seemed so bleak. Through God's miraculous intervention, God favored both Ruth and Naomi.

Ruth married a rich relative and Naomi was blessed in her later years with a grandson. "Then the women said to Naomi, blessed be the LORD, who has not left you this day without a close relative; and may His name be famous in Israel! May he, *the grandson,* be to you a restorer of life and a nourisher of your old age" Ruth 4:14-15 (NKJ) (*emphasis mine.)* The son who was born to Ruth and Boaz was named

Obed, who was the father of Jesse and the grandfather of King David. How well our Father looks after His widows.

God loves aged fruit! Psalm 92:13-15a (NKJ) reads, "Those who are planted in the house of the LORD shall flourish in the courts of our God. They shall still bear fruit in old age; they shall be fresh and flourishing; to declare that the LORD is upright." How He blesses these special ones with rich lives and fond memories. These wonderful palms will line the courts of God! How that blesses me because I am one of them!

Personal Note:

Since I am now among the "aged fruit," although I am not a widow, I am honored to be allowed to serve Him and continue to grow and produce more fruit for His kingdom. In my prayer journal, I have many people for whom I pray. Among them are fourteen widows. I just added the fourteenth one last week, Vivian. I am so blessed to be able to do this.

God is giving me a special heart for widows. How I love them! I do not know why, but I pray God's blessing on every one. This cluster of aged fruit has time to be prayer warriors and intercessors. It is a quiet ministry but one that God cherishes as much as He cherishes each one who is praying.

Prayer:

Father, my heart is so full as I think of Your cherished ones, those who no longer have their husbands by their side. Bless them richly and minister to their needs, in Jesus' precious name, Amen.

Your Reflections:

Day 91

God is . . . Our Father

Bible Reading: I John 3:1-6

The Apostle John spoke more about our Father than any other writer in the New Testament. I cannot help but wonder if that is one of the things that Jesus loved so much about John. It could be why John was set aside to be the one to see the visions of the end-times; He saw heaven and God sitting on His throne with Jesus at His right side. John was the one who portrayed Jesus as the Son of God. That is not to say that he was more important than any of the other disciples, but I think John had a very clear idea of how the kingdom of God worked.

John's overall message in his books always points us to the love of God and how we can become children of God through Jesus Christ, God's Son. John wrote, "How great is the love the Father has lavished on us, that we should be called children of God" I John 3:1 (NIV). God is the epitome of love. Love is the ultimate message of who Christ is. Jesus lived so that we could know God's love. He died and rose from the grave so that we could be a part of that love. How our Father lavishes His love on us! It is limitless, just waiting for us to allow Him to fill us with Himself.

Personal Note:

When I started my quest to know the Father better, little did I realize the depth of His love. When we become intimate with our Father, He thrives on lavishing us with His love, joy, peace, grace, mercy, understanding, righteousness, and provision. I am just beginning to experience the depth of what He has for me. Yesterday, June 14, 2006, I went on a one-day fast and prayer observance. This was the one-year anniversary of my leg being healed. When I decided to do this, I wanted to include as many other people's needs as possible. I cannot begin to tell you what a blessing it was for me.

Last year, when I fasted for the very first time, it was directed more toward my healing. Even though I prayed for many people along with my personal request, healing was the emphasis that God had for me that day.

This was so different. I was very heavy-hearted as I prayed for the needs of about forty people. It made me aware of so many situations and hurts that are all around me. It was prayer for people's need for direction and peace in decision. It was for healing of broken spirits, for spiritual growth, for unknown futures. It was joy mixed with sadness, because I was praying for some very deep hurts. It was blessing amidst sorrow for lost loved ones, it was healing for bodies wracked with disease and pain.

My body ached with the load of these few people, my head throbbed and my throat hurt from the tears that I shed, but far above all of that, was the blessing and the honor of being able to do such a small thing for my Father. I caught just a tiny glimmer, like a grain of sand, of what it must have been like for our Savior to carry the sins, the guilt, and the shame of the whole world on that agonizing day on the cross.

Prayer:

Thank you, my Father, for the joy of serving You. Thank you that because I am Your child, I can bring any request to You and You will hear it and answer it in Your timing, and for Your purpose. You are the God who heals broken lives and deep hurts. Help me to trust You more, even with things that I think are too small. Nothing is unimportant to You! How I worship You and love You! In the powerful name of Jesus, Amen.

Your Reflections:

****

Edwards Brothers, Inc.
Thorofare, NJ USA
January 16, 2012